HOSPITABLE HEALTHCARE™

Hospitable Healthcare™

Just What the **Patient** Ordered!

How Hospitality Can Improve
the Patient Experience

STOWE SHOEMAKER, Ph.D.
PETER YESAWICH, Ph.D.

Hospitable Healthcare: Just What the Patient Ordered!

© 2023 by Stowe Shoemaker, PhD, and Peter C. Yesawich, PhD

Library of Congress Control Number: 2023906908
ISBN: 978-1-954676-50-3 (paperback) 978-1-954676-51-0 (hardcover)
     978-1-954676-51-0 (ebook)

Although this publication is designed to provide accurate information about the subject matter, the publisher and the author assume no responsibility for any errors, inaccuracies, omissions, or inconsistencies herein. This publication is intended as a resource; however, it is not intended as a replacement for direct and personalized professional services.

This publication contains numerous figures. We (Hospitable Healthcare Partners, LLC) hold the copyright for the majority, where indicated, and obtained permission to use the others as follows: Figure 4.1 – Inn at the Market; Figure 4.3 – Skyline Art; Figure 4.4 – Torrance Medical Center; Figure 4.5 – Carpenter, Sellers, Del Gatto; Figures 4.7 and 4.8 – University of California, San Francisco; Figure 4.9 – Marta Zaraska; Figure 6.4 – Medallia, Inc.

Editors: Marci Carson, Deborah Froese
Cover and Interior Design: Emma Elzinga
Graphics Designer: Craig Granger

Printed in the United States of America
First Edition

3 West Garden Street, Ste. 718
Pensacola, FL 32502
www.indigoriverpublishing.com

Ordering Information:
Quantity sales: Special discounts are available on quantity purchases by corporations, associations, and others. For details, contact the publisher at the address above. Orders by US trade bookstores and wholesalers: Please contact the publisher at the address above.

With Indigo River Publishing, you can always expect great books, strong voices, and meaningful messages. Most importantly, you'll always find . . . *words worth reading.*

Contents

Introduction

WE ALL HAVE A STORY about a healthcare experience gone wrong. Sometimes it has to do with the clinical outcome. Oftentimes it's about our frustration with the challenge of getting an appointment, clinic wait times, or bills we didn't expect. But most of the time it's about how poorly we were treated. Yet, the service aspects of any encounter with healthcare providers have the greatest impact on patient satisfaction.

Given that hospitality and healthcare share many common points of customer engagement, we began to wonder why healthcare service providers don't utilize many of the service strategies practiced by hospitality service providers to improve the patient experience. Especially when the data are painfully clear: consumers are much more satisfied by their experiences with hospitality than with healthcare service providers.

Having spent many years working with both hospitality and healthcare service providers, we decided to develop a practical model that would enable healthcare providers to adopt select principles practiced by hospitality providers to enhance the patient experience. It reflects our collective resume from working with some of the most successful hospitality brands: Hilton, Fairmont, Four Seasons, Leading Hotels of the World, Marriott, Ritz-Carlton, CanyonRanch, Disney Parks and Resorts, Landry's Restaurants, Il Fornaio, Taco Bell, ClubCorp; and two of the most admired brands in healthcare: Cancer Treatment Centers of America Global®, and the University of Texas MD Anderson Cancer Center (MDACC).

But we also wanted to share more than just our opinions. So before we started writing this book, we surveyed 1,200 adults in the US to measure their perception of the importance of 24 points of service delivery common to both industries. We had them rate their experiences with each of five types of providers: hotels/resorts, restaurants, hospitals, walk-in clinics, and physicians' offices, hereinafter referred to as our *Gap Survey*. Respondents had visited all five types of providers in 2019, the year prior to the COVID pandemic. We thought we would find some meaningful differences in satisfaction but had no idea just how significant the gaps would be.

Along the way, we also interviewed 25 leading hospitality and healthcare professionals on specific topics. Highlights of our conversations appear as sidebars throughout the book. We think you'll find their comments provocative. It's interesting to note that all of interview subjects expressed agreement with our thesis that healthcare service providers could learn a great deal about how to enhance patient satisfaction from their colleagues in hospitality.

Many of the recommendations made in this book will be easy to implement. Others will be more difficult, even controversial. Several challenge conventional wisdom about the way healthcare should be delivered. But the need for improvement in healthcare delivery is palpable, based on the disappointing service delivery scores most healthcare service providers received in our Gap Survey.

To illustrate the difference between a typical healthcare versus hospitality encounter, we begin by contrasting a fictional individual's experience as a patient getting a colonoscopy with his experience as a guest at a resort in Las Vegas several weeks later. Granted, the prospect of undergoing a colonoscopy is unlikely to elicit high fives like the prospect of a weekend in Vegas. But the contrast reveals many ways the former could be improved by lessons learned from the latter. Both encounters included common steps or services, yet our fictional individual's residual sentiment about each was dramatically different. This shouldn't be the case.

Throughout this book, we discuss the different strategies hospitality service providers have used to enhance the guest experience. We show how healthcare service providers may implement the same techniques to enhance the patient experience. We are confident that practitioners who are inspired to embrace our recommendations will be applauded by patients for their effort—and rewarded by patient loyalty.

Let's begin the journey.

CHAPTER 1

The Need for Hospitable Healthcare

"Hospitality is present when something happens for you. It is absent when something happens to you. Those two simple prepositions – for and to –express it all."

- DANNY MEYER, FOUNDER OF SHAKE SHACK

You're Just a Number Here

MEET ROGER CONWAY, fictional healthcare patient. Roger, 47 years of age, built a successful insurance brokerage that specializes in sourcing competitive home and auto policies for residents of his small Ohio town. Married with two children still living at home, he is in good health (except for the few extra pounds he gained last Thanksgiving) and has visited his primary care physician for an annual physical since his 45th birthday. At the conclusion of Roger's most recent physical, his physician recommended he have a colonoscopy as part of a healthy aging plan. He was referred to the local gastroenterologist, Dr. Garcia, who has performed the procedure in his outpatient clinic for many years. Roger was instructed to make an appointment with Dr. Garcia, which is where his less-than-hospitable healthcare experience began.

Anxious about his first colonoscopy because of reports from buddies about the unpleasant preparation required and risks associated with the discovery of suspicious-looking polyps, Roger decided to research both the doctor and his clinic before scheduling an appointment. The results were a bit concerning. The information on Dr.

Garcia's website was helpful, yet his ratings on Healthgrades.com were mixed, and there were several comments on social media about the abrupt style he and his staff had with patients. He decided to book the appointment anyway. Finding another clinic would require him to travel out of town for the procedure, something he wished to avoid.

When Roger called Dr. Garcia's office, he was greeted by an interactive voice response (IVR) message instructing him to press a specific number to make an appointment. Having done so, he was advised that his call was now in a queue and a member of the "care team" would be with him shortly. While Roger waited, he listened to a recorded message that stated repeatedly how important his call was, and that the doctor's staff was committed to providing exceptional patient care. Several minutes later, he was greeted with a rushed salutation by a live voice on the other end of the line.

Roger explained that he was calling to schedule a colonoscopy at the suggestion of his primary care physician. The anonymous female voice asked him to confirm his name, date of birth, social security number, and what appeared to be the item of greatest interest to the scheduler: his medical insurance. She then stated their first opening was in four weeks at 8:00 a.m., a day in which Roger had booked important appointments with clients that would be difficult to change.

Clearly annoyed by Roger's lack of availability on the date that was convenient for the clinic, the scheduler reluctantly asked Roger for some days and times that he would be available. They settled on a date approximately five weeks later. She then recited some information about how he should prepare for the procedure and sent Roger a perfunctory email with specific instructions on what to do in anticipation of his arrival that day.

The evening prior to his appointment had been rather unpleasant, but Roger understood it was just part of the preparation necessary to facilitate the procedure. Accompanied by his wife, to provide a sense of comfort and a return ride home after emerging from the haze of the anesthetic, flashbacks to comments made by his buddies elevated

Roger's anxiety about the upcoming procedure. *What happens if the doctor finds something that looks suspicious? What if the procedure goes awry and my colon is perforated? Will my insurance cover the cost? How long will it take for me to feel normal again?*

The greeting at Dr. Garcia's office was surprising and not particularly welcoming. Roger began with a pleasant "good morning" to which the receptionist gave a cursory reply, and he had to remind her why he was there. She immediately got down to business, asking Roger for his name, date of birth, and medical insurance card. The glass partition separating the two amplified the emotional distance between them. Eye contact was fleeting. The somber expression on the receptionist's face signaled the tone of the event that would soon follow.

Roger was given a clipboard populated with numerous pages of questions, many of which could have been answered ahead of time had his primary care physician sent the requested information to Dr. Garcia's office. After completing his documentation, Roger sat quietly in the patient waiting room as his uneasiness continued to build. Finally, a nurse emerged from a door at the corner of the room and, loudly enough for all in the waiting area to hear, she announced: "Roger Conway."

His time had come.

Roger was led into a semi-private area, told to undress, don the gown folded neatly on the bed, and lie down. The situation reminded him of his first day in the armed forces when he exchanged his civilian clothes for his military attire. Appropriately gowned and ready to go, Roger watched the ceiling roll by as he was wheeled from the prep room to the procedure room where he met Dr. Garcia for the first time. He greeted Roger with a brief "hello-ready-to-get-started" in a manner that suggested there wasn't any time for chit-chat because the team needed to remain on schedule for what would assuredly be another busy day. After listening to a few words about the anesthetic and recovery procedure, Roger succumbed to the anesthetic.

When he awoke, Roger was pleased to see his wife and yet another medical professional he did not recognize from either the reception or procedure rooms. The fog in his head had cleared sufficiently for him to ask the all-important questions: "How did it go? Everything okay?"

Of course, the nurse was not authorized to discuss results with patients. She told them that Dr. Garcia's office would be in touch with the results in a few days. Roger relinquished his gown, gathered his belongings, and worried all the way home.

Good news arrived a few days later; there were no signs of any suspicious growths. The only follow-up required would be another colonoscopy in about ten years. But concerning news arrived a few weeks later. Even though he was not made aware at the time of scheduling—or at check in—Roger discovered his insurance would not cover the entire cost. First, he received an invoice in the mail from Dr. Garcia's office totaling almost $750, an expense he hadn't planned on when he booked the procedure. A few days later, another unexpected bill arrived, this time from the anesthesiologist for the equivalent of his monthly mortgage payment. And upon further reflection, Roger wondered why Dr. Garcia's office had never solicited his feedback on the entire experience.

We're Glad You're Here

Meet Roger Conway, hotel guest.

Two months post-colonoscopy, Roger and his wife decided they needed a break from the demands of their respective daily obligations. They had accumulated quite a few reward points from credit card purchases over the previous year, and hotels in Las Vegas were promoting attractive deals. The couple went online to explore the options, compare prices, check availability, and watch videos of four different resorts at which they could redeem their points. They booked a deluxe room with a breathtaking view of the Vegas Strip at night.

Roger was a member of the brand's loyalty program, so the resort had his profile information and stay preferences on file. Upon arrival, he and his wife were greeted at the reception desk by name. The only thing required at registration was proper identification. Because of his loyalty, he was surprised and delighted to learn the resort receptionist had upgraded them to a junior suite—at no extra cost.

Once settled in their elegant suite, Roger and his wife began planning which of the special dining and entertainment offers, received prior to arrival, they would choose for their visit.

Four enjoyable days and three wonderful nights later, it was time to head back to Ohio. After Roger reviewed and settled their bill on his mobile phone app, they walked to the hotel entrance. Their bellman had already loaded their luggage into an awaiting taxi to the airport.

Bidding them a fond farewell, the smartly attired doorman asked if they enjoyed their visit and added, "We're looking forward to welcoming the Conways back again soon."

Two days later, while sitting in his office in Ohio, Roger received an email from the hotel manager thanking him for his business, requesting feedback on his stay, and extending a warm invitation to return. He was reminded again of the wonderful time he and his wife had in Vegas when reviewing his credit card statement the following month, noting he also earned 2,500 loyalty points to spend on a future trip.

A Stark Contrast

The motivations for Roger Conway's two service experiences were obviously different. Although they shared some commonalities, they resulted in very disparate customer experiences. Why? Because our protagonist's hospitality experience addressed the needs and concerns of the customer, while his healthcare experience focused on the needs and concerns of the service provider.

Consumer sentiment about these two different approaches to service delivery is evident in the degree of satisfaction they express with each of the five types of service providers measured in our Gap Survey as revealed in Figure 1.1. Note: Because respondents rated their hotel/

motel/resort experience highest for most of the attributes tested, all tests of statistical significance have been conducted against the rating for this cohort. Columns appearing in red denote a significant difference from the hotel/motel/resort rating. Refer to Appendix A for a complete list of service attributes tested, their ratings, and corresponding tests of statistical significance.

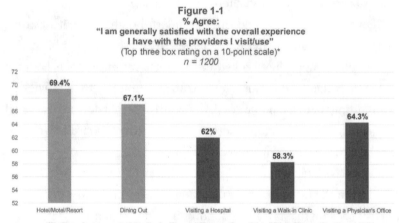

*Red bar denotes a statistically significant difference from "Hotel/Motel/Resort" rating at 95%.

Figure 1.1: Overall satisfaction with five types of service providers.

As reflected in the figure, consumers rate their level of satisfaction with the overall experience provided by hotels, resorts, and restaurants significantly higher than with hospitals, walk-in clinics, and physicians' offices.

When confronted with this reality, many medical professionals are quick to assert their belief about why: the circumstances that often precipitate the need for healthcare services are fundamentally different from those that motivate the consumption of hospitality services. The former generally reflect needs whereas the latter reflect wants. Yet, our data clearly reveal significant gaps in the quality of healthcare service delivery and suggest the adoption of proven hospitality principles would enhance patient satisfaction despite the distinctly different motivations for consumption. The fact that many healthcare services are sought in times of high anxiety and uncertainty amplifies the importance of healthcare providers delivering services in a hospitable manner.

So why does this disparity in the quality of service exist? Staff training and culture certainly contribute. But we believe the root cause for much of the difference in consumer sentiment is simple: the degree of competition that prevails in the hospitality versus healthcare industries.

Growing competition in the hospitality industry forced practitioners to discover and embrace new ways to reach, engage, serve, and then listen to customer feedback. This awareness led the most successful hospitality enterprises to develop comprehensive profiles of customers' preferences and consumption habits which, in turn, enables them to anticipate customer needs and desires, offer more innovative product or service options, recognize and reward customer loyalty, request customer feedback, and then act upon what they learn. Furthermore, most hospitality service providers have accomplished this while making the process of consuming the services they offer easy, even fun.

Can the same be said of most patient encounters with healthcare service providers?

Apparently not, based on the trends observed in the American Customer Satisfaction Index (ACSI). The ACSI is a national cross-industry index of customer satisfaction in the United States. The data in Figure 1.2 reveal the national index (100-point scale) for hospitals in the US between 2010 and 2020 declined four percentage points (from 73% in 2010 to 69% in 2020), while the same index for the best-performing lodging company, Hilton, increased from 80% to 82% during the same period. The 13-point difference between these industry scores in 2020 is noteworthy, but the directional trend over the ten-year term is even more so.[1]

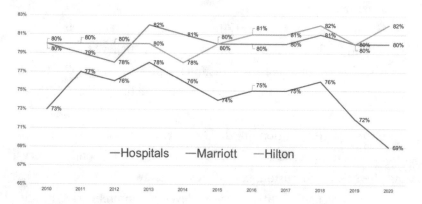

Figure 1.2: American Customer Satisfaction Index for hospitals vs. hotels.

Results for restaurants, the other major component of the hospitality industry, are equally compelling, as revealed in Figure 1.3. Olive Garden, one of the leading brands in the casual dining category, weighed in ten points higher than hospitals in customer satisfaction for 2020. Domino's, a leader in the pizza category, weighed in two points higher over the ten-year term.

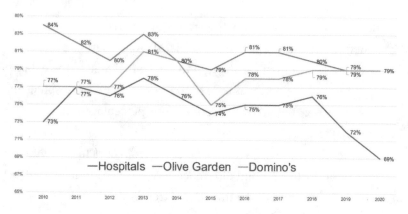

Figure 1.3: American Customer Satisfaction Index for hospitals vs. restaurants.

The observed decline in customer satisfaction with hospital services is particularly vexing given the rising cost of their services.

Specifically, even though the US spent an average of $10,202 per capita on healthcare in 2020,[2] more than any other country, Americans are more dissatisfied with their healthcare system than residents of countries that spend less.[3]

Given that the average annual cost of employer-provided health coverage for a family plan topped $22,000 for the very first time in 2021, one can reasonably assume satisfaction with healthcare in the US has declined further since then.[4]

One thing is abundantly clear: Spending more on the delivery of healthcare, and specifically hospital services, hasn't translated into higher customer/patient satisfaction.

So, what does result in higher customer satisfaction? It is useful to look at prevailing service strategies in the hospitality industry for answers. Why? Because both healthcare and hospitality are service industries, both provide intangible services, and many of the changes occurring in healthcare today began more than 50 years ago in the hospitality industry. And we believe the past is prologue.

The Road Trip That Changed the Hospitality Industry

The story begins in 1951 when Kemmons Wilson, founder of the Holiday Inn chain of hotels, decided to take his family on a road trip to Washington, DC. He was disappointed—actually, outraged—by the poor quality and lack of consistency in the

Maurie Markman, MD, a distinguished medical oncologist, is President of Medicine and Science at Cancer Treatment Centers of America Global, Inc. (CTCA), part of City of Hope. He calls himself a "people's doctor" who is committed to offering patients every evidence-based option available to beat their disease.

"Hospitality and healthcare are very different when it comes to the role of the purchaser versus the consumer. In hospitality, the purchaser is the consumer. Healthcare is exactly the opposite because patients rarely pay the bill. Rather, they pay a premium to an insurer who then pays a negotiated rate for the bill. Therefore, the delivery of healthcare is not a customer-friendly experience."

roadside accommodations he encountered as he traveled north from Memphis to the nation's capital.[5] While traveling, he developed a list of features he felt should be part of any hotel stay, such as standardized room size, free in-room television, direct-dial telephones, and so on. So inspired, he collaborated with a draftsman to draw up plans for his first hotel. The draftsman had recently watched the movie *Holiday Inn* starring Bing Crosby; hence, the first global lodging brand was born, and the hospitality industry began a transformation that continues today.

A key to the Holiday Inn brand's success was the standardization of its product so customers knew what to expect prior to reserving a room whenever they stayed at a Holiday Inn, regardless of location. In 1975, executives at Holiday Inn coined an advertising slogan to communicate the essence of this promise: "The best surprise is no surprise."[6]

A hotel stay, like many services, is consumed at the same time it is purchased; that means there is no opportunity to "try before you buy." This is referred to as *simultaneous production and consumption* and occurs whenever customers purchase a product at the same time they consume the product. Unlike a physical product such as a car, which you can take for a test drive prior to purchase, you cannot touch or feel a service before buying it. By creating a standardized guest experience with a common brand name, Wilson attempted—successfully—to let customers know exactly what they were buying prior to spending a night at a Holiday Inn, thereby making it easier to evaluate the expected quality of the service prior to purchase.

Dr. Leonard Berry is a Distinguished Professor of Marketing at Texas A&M University and a widely published author on the science of service quality with a focus on healthcare.

"Healthcare is a "need" service, while hospitality is a "want" service. This important distinction defines the unique state-of-mind that prevails when individuals consume each type of service. Yet, healthcare service providers can reduce patient anxiety and improve the overall patient experience by adopting many of the service principles of hospitality."

Getting To Know You

While Wilson made it easy for guests to know what to expect when they stayed at a Holiday Inn, others in the hospitality industry realized it was equally important for Holiday Inn, or any other hospitality service provider, to know as much about their guests as their guests knew about their properties. Hospitality executives came to realize the more they knew about guests' wants, needs, and desires, the easier it would be to provide them with a great experience. And, importantly, an experience that could not be replicated easily by other hospitality service providers with similar accommodations.

Consider Roger Conway, our fictional patient. He and his wife had a great vacation in Las Vegas because they stayed in a resort that knew a lot about Roger and his preferences. They knew this because he was a member of the brand's loyalty program. As a member of that program, Roger had given the brand permission to keep track of his preferences—from room type to bedding, pillows, and more—so they could meet his expectations every time he stayed with that brand. Contrast this with a typical visit to a healthcare service provider during which one is usually asked to provide much of the same information upon each visit.

The great independent hotels kept a guest book that detailed important information about their guests. But these insights only benefited guests when they stayed at that hotel. As hospitality companies began franchising their brands to different owners in different cities, they needed a way for every branded property to know more about the preferences of guests, even if those guests had never stayed with them before. The creation and tracking of guest profiles through the introduction of customer relationship management (CRM) programs was the answer. We discuss this topic in greater detail in chapter three.

Figure 1.4 shows the transition from the guest knowing a lot about the brand to the brand knowing a lot about the guest. On the far left, the brand knows nothing about the guest. However, because of brand standardization initially championed by Kemmons Wilson, the guest now knows a great deal about the product or service provided by the brand. At the far right, the brand knows a lot about the guest because the guest has given the brand permission to collect information about their stay and related preferences in exchange for special recognition. The guest receives better service as a result. Guests may also be rewarded for their patronage through such things as discounts, free upgrades, loyalty points, access to special events, and the like. We discuss these strategies in greater detail in chapter seven.

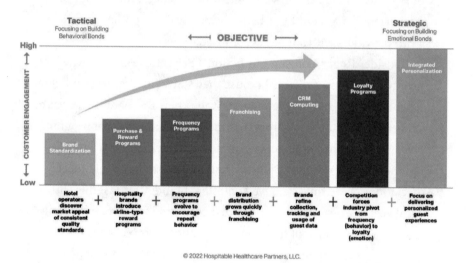

Figure 1.4: Evolution of guest engagement in the hospitality industry.

The transition from knowing very little about guests to knowing a great deal did not happen overnight, of course. Rather, it took place as guests became more willing to exchange information about themselves for perks. We believe a similar transition will occur in the healthcare industry, yet at a much faster pace because of consumers' access to and use of evolving technology, and their demonstrated affection for customer recognition and reward programs.

Service providers now regularly motivate guests to provide more extensive information on travel habits or preferences through *gamification*. In exchange for extra points, miles, or other rewards, guests are usually willing to buy more product or behave in certain ways. Providers are more than happy to fund this quid pro quo, realizing the value they receive by collecting customer preference and behavior data.

Gamification started in the 1950s and 1960s. During that time, many people collected S&H Green Stamps when they made a qualifying purchase. They could redeem those stamps for gifts, with each gift "sold" for a given number of stamps. United Airlines adapted the essence of this idea to the airline business in the early 1970. They recognized frequent passengers by conferring plaques and other rewards. American Airlines raised the bar for customer recognition with the introduction of its now legendary AAdvantage® Program in 1981 by offering special fares to frequent flyers. They migrated to a "miles flown" compensation formula that serves as the foundation for most frequent flyer programs today.

The Holiday Inn and Marriott chains created the first hotel loyalty programs in 1983. Recognizing the appeal of these programs to customers, astute marketers in practically every other retail industry began introducing similar programs. So, today, customers—guests—are equally likely to participate in an airline frequent flyer program, a hotel chain frequent stay program, a Starbucks Rewards program, and several retailers' frequent shopper programs, perhaps even one sponsored by their local car wash.

The advent of the computer revolution made capturing and storing massive amounts of data on customers both cheap and efficient. Suddenly, the guest book created by a single general manager in a hotel could be shared electronically across multiple hotels. The evolving sophistication of this effort allowed management of the Las Vegas resort to provide Roger with a wonderful experience, even though he had never visited that location before.

As customer recognition programs have matured, one thing has become increasingly clear: Personalization of the guest experience is critical to enhancing guest satisfaction in both hospitality and healthcare because both are service industries. Yes, the services are fundamentally different in scope, purpose, and outcome, but their methods of delivery are very similar. Both are essentially intangible. It is hard to touch and feel them prior to purchase.

Thanks to Kemmons Wilson and the many prescient executives who followed him, the hospitality industry realized that many travelers use cues to evaluate the quality of services they receive. In Wilson's day, cues were considered novel for the time: free in-room TV, direct-dial phones, daily maid service, and a common brand name called "Holiday Inn," which signified that the hotel had all these amenities. Wilson also showed that by providing customers with what they expected, they were more likely to leave satisfied which, in turn, increased the probability of returning at some future date.

Academic research on customer satisfaction in the early 1990s revealed that satisfaction was a function of how well service delivery aligned with customers' expectations. If the service equaled expectations, satisfaction resulted. If the service exceeded expectations, satisfaction also resulted. If, however, the service fell below expectations, dissatisfaction typically followed. (Much of the academic research on services, which we discuss below, was developed in the 1990s and is covered in the textbook by Wirtz and Lovelock, 2016.[7])

So how do you define the components of a service, given their intangible nature? What causes the difference between service performance and expectation? And how are service expectations formed?

We answer these three questions throughout *Hospitable Healthcare*. At the same time, Figures 1.2 and 1.3 explain why Marriott, Hilton, Olive Garden, and Dominos enjoy higher customer satisfaction scores than hospitals year-over-year, and how providers in the healthcare industry may achieve scores equal to or higher than those enjoyed by the hospitality industry. But first, it is useful to present a framework that helps one understand how to answer these three questions.

Figure 1.5 reveals the four components of a service.[8] The first is the physical product, something customers can touch and feel. The physical product cues customers to the level of quality. For example, hotels use white bedspreads to enhance guests' perception of guest room cleanliness. Clean bathrooms in hotels and restaurants are cues suggesting the front of the house is so clean and well appointed that the kitchen must be the same. Therefore, healthcare service providers should ask themselves two questions about the cues their facilities provide: What physical cues serve as quality proxies for patients? Are we providing these cues in an appropriate way? For example, consider the state of restrooms. What does a dirty restroom signify compared to a clean restroom? Which organization has a cleaner back of the house?

Second, service is equivalent to a performance purchased by the guest. Hospitality service providers talk about "planning your work" just as one would plan a performance. Management should develop and plan every action undertaken by employees when they interact with guests. Consideration is given to the personal attributes of employees, such as friendliness, speed, attitude, professionalism, and responsiveness. But other factors are important as well. Some may depend on employee aptitude but also on service protocols developed by the organization, such as how guests are greeted. Others may depend strictly on management decisions, such as when to offer guests a complimentary beverage or an upgrade to nicer accommodations if or when service failures occur.

Third, the service delivery refers to what happens when customers consume the service. Hospitality executives talk about "working your plan." That is, performing all the steps that were developed before the guest arrives. The all-important moment of truth (described later) happens when the service product meets the service delivery.

And fourth, the service environment, also known as the *servicescape*, describes the "physical environment in which the service is delivered."[9] The three distinct elements that comprise the service environments are: ambient physical conditions, spatial layout, and signage and symbols.

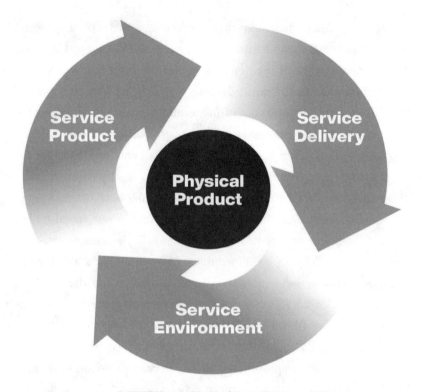

© 2022 Hospitable Healthcare Partners, LLC.

Figure 1.5: The four components of service.

1. Ambient physical conditions are created by such things as architecture, lighting, background music, and decor.

2. The spatial layout may also create a certain atmosphere. For instance, one casino in Las Vegas purposely made the walkways narrow so customers would rub shoulders with each other while transitioning through them.

3. Signage and symbols, the third element of the service environment, should concern both hospitality and healthcare executives. A lack of signage—or confusing signage—can easily create feelings of chaos and disorientation. Signs not only direct customers, but they may also be used to inform customers about procedures.

In reference to the third point, Shoemaker recalls standing in line for about 15 minutes waiting to get into a restaurant only to learn, when he reached the hostess stand, that he was not in line for admission to the restaurant, but to purchase the restaurant's promotional merchandise. To his dismay, he discovered there was no line waiting to get into the restaurant, and no sign pointing customers seeking entry to the restaurant in the right direction.

During a recent Saturday visit to a hospital in Las Vegas to visit a patient, Shoemaker decided to use the valet service because the only convenient parking spots available were reserved for valet or physicians. He followed the valet signs, but no one was there. He then parked in front of the hospital, ran in to the reception area to inquire as to the whereabouts of the attendant and was told the valet only worked Monday to Friday, 8:00 a.m. to 5:00 p.m. When asked where to park, given the only empty parking spots were reserved for physicians, the receptionist said, "I guess you can park in the spots reserved for valet. Just move the cones to get in."

Now that we understand the components of a service, we can begin to examine the potential gaps in service delivery and where they may occur.[10] Figure 1.6 reveals the five reasons these gaps occur.

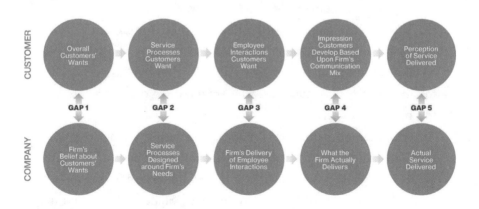

© 2022 Hospitable Healthcare Partners, LLC.

Figure 1.6: Key determinants of service gaps.

GAP ONE

This refers to the discrepancy between what service providers believe are customers' wants and needs, and their actual wants and needs. This gap occurs because clear communication is lacking between customers and management, and between contact employees and managers. For example, customers may communicate their wants and needs to employees in general conversation, but there is no mechanism for these comments to ascend the chain of command. As such, the information may remain with the employee and never be shared with management.

This gap also occurs when there is inadequate customer research. Many companies simply do not ask customers about their wants, needs, expectations or problems; rather, they assume they already know.

GAP TWO

This occurs when the service provider fails to design service procedures that meet the expectations of guests. This is often caused by an operationally driven mentality, which is knowing what guests want but not providing it because operational concerns take priority. This mentality is reflected in the pejorative phrase, "This would be a great business if the customers didn't get in the way."

This also occurs because the reward system for employees' conflicts with the needs of guests. For instance, managers who are rewarded based on meeting their budget will be less likely to go over-budget to satisfy guests than managers who are rewarded on **both** adherence to a budget **and** measures of overall satisfaction.

A final reason for this gap is a poor service design. When Shoemaker asked a food service waiter why it took so long to be served, the waiter replied, "We closed the kitchen next to this dining area to save money. Now I have to walk all the way to the main kitchen, which is on the other side of the building."

GAP THREE

This gap occurs when the staff does not implement management's plan. One of the main reasons for this gap is a poor human resources policy. A poor policy leads to hiring "warm bodies," as opposed to the right person for the job. It also leads to an unwillingness to properly train employees and poor scheduling of employees. Ironically, if too many employees are on duty, service may suffer because every employee thinks it is someone else's job to serve the customer. If too few employees are working relative to the demand, service may also suffer because attention is lacking.

GAP FOUR

This is the gap between service expected and service delivered. It occurs because advertising or sales presentations for the services misrepresent what the provider can deliver. Overzealous marketing is frequently the culprit. For example, to make their service appealing, hotel companies often include a picture of their largest and nicest guest rooms, even if most of the available rooms look quite different from the one featured in the brochure. They frequently show very attractive men and women lounging by the pool, even though actual guests present in a decidedly different manner.

Finally, aggressive hotel salespeople may say anything to get the business from group meeting and convention planners. They "sell the dream," and then the operations team must "live the nightmare."

GAP FIVE

This occurs between customers' perceptions of service delivered and the actual service delivered when they are disgruntled by the other four gaps. This can occur even when the first four conditions appear perfect. Customers tend to forget when their expectations are met and remember when they are not, since much of the service experience is intangible. Because customers don't always recognize when service providers have delivered as promised, they must be reminded they are, in fact, receiving great service. Reminders may be created by manipulating the five dimensions of service quality: *Reliability, Assurance, Tangibility, Empathy, and Responsiveness.* These five dimensions are often referred to by the acronym RATER. By including one or more of these dimensions in every customer interaction, customers are reminded that they're receiving quality.

So how does the RATER system work? Consider a hotel's in-room dining experience. The hotelier's goal is to have guests recommend the in-room dining experience to their friends. Employing the RATER system can remind guests that they have received excellent service. Here is a description of the RATER system in practice for that service:

Reliability

- When the guest calls in an order, the phone is answered within three rings.
- The room service waiter or waitress carries all the accompaniments a guest could reasonably request and tells the guest that he or she is prepared to accommodate any additional requests.

Assurance

- The order is repeated at the time it is received and repeated once again when the order is delivered.
- The person taking the order is familiar with all the items on the menu and may therefore answer any questions asked.

Tangibility

- The room service dining menu is wiped clean after each use and presented to each guest without food stains or fingerprints.
- The tray on which the food is served is spotless. Fine hotels and resorts accessorize the tray with an aromatic flower to amplify the sense of freshness.

- Dirty trays are picked up immediately after the guest has dined and not left in the hallway until the next morning.

Empathy

- The person taking the order truly listens to the guest's requests and, when appropriate, makes comments to illustrate he or she is listening. For instance, if a guest mentions great thirst, the staff person says, "I'll be sure to add extra ice water to your order." Or if the guest mentions deep hunger, the staff person responds by saying, "I'll put a rush on your order."

Responsiveness:

- Instead of saying, "Your food will be delivered in 30 minutes," staff will say, "It is now 10:00 p.m., and your food will be delivered by 10:30 p.m." This sets a beginning and end time for the service. Without these parameters, it is hard for the guest to know if the food was delivered on time and effectively evaluate service quality. When the employee delivers the food, they should review the order with the guest and then ask, "What time would you like your dishes picked up?"

Reflect for a moment on how Roger Conway's recent colonoscopy experience could have improved through application of the RATER concept. Although unlikely to compare favorably against his fond memory of the weekend in Vegas, there were certainly several opportunities for the clinic to enhance his experience prior, during, and after his visit. See the Appendix B for an example of how the RATER system could have applied to Roger's colonoscopy.

So how are guests' expectations formed? Understanding the various stimuli that coalesce to create expectations enables service providers to influence them. As referenced in the discussion of Gap Four, this is critical. Figure 1.7 reveals the different sources of information that contribute to the formation of guests' expectations.

© 2022 Hospitable Healthcare Partners, LLC.

Figure 1.7: Key drivers of customer expectations.

Most of the inputs shown in Figure 1.7 are self-explanatory. A few are worth special mention, however. First, as Kemmons Wilson found after his journey to Washington, DC in the 1950s, there was an emerging desire for guests to stay in a hotel that was part of a recognizable brand because brands promised predictable quality. Hence, prior experience with similar types of purchases has a major impact on expectations.

Second, the proliferation of published ratings for practically all services has had an outsized influence on customer expectations, even when the source credibility is questionable.

Third, the ease with which customers may now share comments

on service delivery through social media is unprecedented and contributes to customers' expectations. We examine each of these sources of influence in greater detail later in this book.

So, having set the stage for our journey, in the parlance of healthcare, "The doctor will see you now."

Rick Evans is Senior Vice President and Chief Experience Officer of New York-Presbyterian Hospital. He is responsible for overseeing New York-Presbyterian's efforts to enhance the patient and family experience across the continuum of care along with developing and implementing a comprehensive strategy to increase patient satisfaction and consumer experience across the enterprise.

"The patient experience derives from the arc and quality of interactions between patients and members of the care team . . . from the transporter to the floor nurse, to the treating physician . . . not just select contributors. The sum of these interactions builds patient confidence in the quality of care provided. It must therefore be managed from the first interaction to the last, with each team member trained to communicate in a consistent manner. Because consistency builds confidence, and the patient experience is ultimately determined by the confidence patients have in their care team."

CHAPTER 2

Hospitality in Healthcare: The PAEER Model

"We are drowning in information but starved for knowledge."

– JOHN NAISBITT, AUTHOR AND FUTURIST

What's Wrong with Me, Dr. Google?

IT SEEMS LIKE SYMPTOM-CHECKERS are everywhere today. We have all heard facetious remarks about the influence of "Dr. Google," yet WebMD provides possible diagnoses, even suggested treatment options, for practically any malaise. Just share your age, gender, list of symptoms, and roster of current medications and a possible diagnosis with a list of treatment options appears.

Several major healthcare providers reinforce this trend by offering their own online diagnostic tools. For example, the Cancer Treatment Centers of America Global® risk assessment tool will reveal your risk of a cancer diagnosis if you provide information about your demography, ethnicity, family history, and current or previous consumption of tobacco products. Mayo Clinic ups the ante with a full suite of symptom assessments using an interactive verbal exchange through voice-activated Amazon Alexa Skills allowing you to ask questions such as "Alexa, am I having migraines?"

Given the breadth of information available with just a few key clicks or the sound of your voice, it is no wonder an estimated one out of six adults consult online sources before receiving a formal diagnosis of a

Jeff Arnold is Co-founder, Chairman, and Chief Executive Officer of . Sharecare, a digital health company that helps people manage all their health in one place. He was also the founder of WebMD and serves as Chairman of Forbes Travel Guide.

"Purveyors of healthcare information online must be fluent in three languages: healthcare, technology, and media. And the information they provide must be right 100% of the time to build the confidence of users. It should not be contaminated by unverified information, whether that comes from a designated expert or is user generated.

No two patient experiences in healthcare information websites should be the same. Rather, they should reflect the known healthcare status and aspirations of the individual users to maximize relevance, increase engagement, and ultimately, influence behavior."

specific medical condition.[1] A recent survey of 2,000 adults conducted by personal health testing company, LetsGetChecked, found the percentage of adults who try to diagnose their symptoms through internet searches is a staggering 65%.[2] In the Gap Survey conducted by the authors of this book, fully 71% of respondents attempted to self-diagnose specific symptoms they experienced.

Whether it is 16%, 71%, or somewhere in between, it is clear the "information everywhere" world in which we now live has transformed the way we think about, search for, and engage with healthcare service providers. Yet, unlike the considerable information readily available to consumers on the quality of hospitality service providers such as lodging and dining establishments—think *TripAdvisor*, *Forbes*, AAA, Yelp, OpenTable—feedback on the quality of services provided by the healthcare industry is much harder to come by and, more importantly, harder to interpret.

For example, the more rigorous physician rating services typically require a minimum of 30 individual patient reviews to publish results. Although fake reviews have been a concern of hospitality service providers, prompting many to actively monitor content for authenticity, this has recently emerged as a concern for healthcare service providers as well.[3] Consumer confidence in the veracity of healthcare service provider reviews will certainly diminish if specious reviews become more common.

Contrast the limited availability of healthcare provider ratings—whether for hospitals or physicians—with the plethora of ratings one can find online for most hospitality service providers. A significant part of this gap may be explained by the fact that many healthcare service providers fail to ask patients to provide feedback on their experiences, and therefore, have none to share. Patients' reticence about dissing a medical professional publicly online may be another reason these quality assessments are not as plentiful as one might expect. Such reticence does not dissuade guests from opining about hospitality service providers who fail to deliver, however. When a restaurant ruins an anniversary dinner, or a hotel bungles a wedding reception, the internet is typically set ablaze with negative commentary.

Although this transparency may be painful for the providers, we believe it is one of the reasons hospitality service providers enjoy higher customer satisfaction than healthcare service providers, as revealed in the preceding chapter. Previous customers tell it like it is, so future customers know what to expect.

Differences in the sentiments expressed about hospitality versus healthcare service providers were revealed in our Gap Survey. They appear in a series of tables presented throughout the rest of this book and on our website, hospitablehealthcare.com. The most positive ratings on all but two of the 24 points of service engagement were observed for staying in a hotel/motel/resort. For that reason, we have compared the hotel/motel/resort ratings with the other industry ratings on each variable to determine any statistically significant differences and, where observed, highlight these differences in the figures in red.

As revealed in our Gap Survey, consumers are reluctant to express dissatisfaction with poor service from all healthcare service providers, especially hospitals. Only 54% do so when the service they receive from hospitals is unsatisfactory. Essentially the same percentage (55%) do so when they have an unsatisfactory experience at a walk-in clinic.

Yet fully 61% register their dissatisfaction with hotels/resorts, and 59% do the same for restaurants that disappoint.

We surmise the reticence to express dissatisfaction with healthcare service providers is attributable to two things. First, most of us have been raised to display appropriate respect for medical professionals because of their extensive training and commitment to our well-being. Second, and perhaps more importantly, most patients lack the sufficient contextual knowledge to evaluate the quality of clinical services received, unlike the context most consumers possess for the evaluation of a hotel stay or meal in a restaurant.

Guests of hotels and resorts approach transactions with providers in a far more enlightened manner, however, because of their tendency to access and review available information about hospitality service providers. For example, according to the MMGY Global *Portrait of American Travelers*®, two thirds of travelers consult provider-specific ratings on TripAdvisor before booking a hotel, motel, or resort.[4]

A similar pattern is evident among patrons of full-service restaurants: According to pollster GatherUp, over 58% of consumers use reviews to help select restaurants at least one quarter of the time; and 36% use reviews to inform their selection half the time or more.[5]

Hospitality service providers have learned that transparency about performance is a good thing. It helps inform guests about the choices they make, the suppliers they select, and the service they can expect. It also enables providers to champion legitimate claims of superior performance with credibility, and it provides a plausible basis for brand differentiation. Superior performance confirmed through transparent ratings also enhances pricing power: the ability to charge and receive a premium price. In short, transparency about performance yields a win-win for customers and providers alike.

One therefore wonders why so few healthcare service providers have adopted a similar posture with respect to the solicitation and publication of feedback on the services they provide. The same question applies to the compilation and publication of information on the clinical outcomes they achieve, which would help patients make more enlightened choices about their healthcare. We believe these disclosures will become inevitable as the "information everywhere" paradigm evolves.

So why do service providers in the hospitality industry appear much more focused on the solicitation and utilization of customer feedback than those in healthcare? Part of the difference may be explained by the more guest-centric culture of the hospitality industry; after all, it purveys hospitality. Or perhaps the hospitality industry's more rapid adoption and integration of technology enables guests to share opinions and other information about providers and services more easily.

Alas, we believe there is an even more basic reason for the disparity observed in the value ascribed to customer feedback by the two industries, as cited earlier: the presence—or absence— of competition. Most hospitality service providers operate in highly competitive markets, but many healthcare providers do not. Companies and practitioners who wish to provide hospitality services typically gravitate to markets where demand for their service is greatest, thereby increasing competition for the addressable demand in those markets.

Conversely, companies and practitioners who wish to provide healthcare services in a specific geographic market are typically subject to legal or policy regulations that constrain competition. These include such things as certificates of need for healthcare facilities, strictures imposed by regulators who control the licensing of facilities, and payors who decide which service providers will be included in their networks and how much they will be paid for the services they provide. The necessity for customer feedback is not as compelling in these less-competitive environments.

The Price/Quality Conundrum

For consumers of both hospitality and healthcare services, however, there is a fundamental belief that superior quality justifies a premium price. Further, there is a common belief that price is an accurate indicator of the quality of the product or service to be consumed. Yet, this presumed relationship appears more applicable to hospitality than healthcare service providers.

For example, the hospitality industry frequently conducts pricing research to understand price/quality relationships and elasticity of demand. When Taco Bell accelerated its growth phase, it had to address a very basic question: what was the appropriate price for a soft taco? To answer this question, they conducted primary research in which they asked consumers five questions:[6]

1. At what price would a soft taco be so expensive you would not buy it?

2. At what price would a soft taco be expensive, but you would buy it?

3. At what price would a soft taco be so cheap that you would worry about the quality?

4. At what price would a soft taco be cheap, but you would not worry about the quality?

5. What price would you expect to pay for a soft taco?

The research revealed the ideal price for a single soft taco. Once determined, Taco Bell redesigned the business processes required to profitably produce and market soft tacos.

Shoemaker recently asked similar questions when advising the administrator in charge of pricing season tickets for the University of Nevada, Las Vegas (UNLV) NCAA football games at the new Allegiant Stadium, also home to the Las Vegas Raiders NFL team. The questions pertained to the view of the field based on the seat location. The answers were used to determine what to charge for seats in different locations in the stadium.

Perhaps not surprisingly, the results revealed that willingness to pay declined as one moved away from the center of field and higher up in the stands. While this may seem intuitive, the value of the research revealed the perceived difference between expensive and "cheap" seats. The resulting pricing strategy enabled UNLV to adopt a pricing strategy that generated more revenue than initially projected while also reflecting the sentiments of fans.

The relationship between price and quality is particularly relevant in both the hospitality and healthcare industries because the services provided are intangible. Hence, consumers use external cues such as the price of the service to make assumptions about quality. For example, when evaluating two different hotels located close to each other in the same destination, travelers typically conclude that the one offering accommodations at $300 per night must be superior to the one offering accommodations at $159 per night. Similarly, when evaluating different restaurants to celebrate an anniversary, diners typically conclude a restaurant rated "$$$$" must be more special than one rated "$$."

Does this same logic apply to the evaluation of healthcare services? Clearly not, and for myriad reasons. First, consumers of healthcare services generally do not know the cost of most services before they receive them because prices are not readily available. The US government's Centers for Medicare and Medicaid Services (CMS) is attempting to rectify this, however, something we will discuss later in the book. If a consumer does inquire about healthcare and is quoted a price, that price frequently does not reflect the patient's obligation. When it is offered, there is usually uncertainty about what percentage the purchaser of the healthcare services—typically the insurance company or payor—will cover. Even more perplexing, there is generally no relationship between the price of the service rendered and the clinical outcome. Although the CMS rewards healthcare providers for achieving better clinical outcomes by increasing the value of the payments they receive for the services rendered, the financial incentives for superior performance are a fraction of the billable cost.

The contrast between the hospitality and healthcare industries could not be more black-and-white than on this critical dimension of "pay for performance." If one has a bad night at a reputable hotel, for example, the manager will likely be quick to comp the bill. After sending an unacceptable entrée back to the kitchen in a fine-dining restaurant, an adjustment will likely be made to your check with apologies followed by the unexpected arrival of a complimentary desert. But dare you contest the bill for a surgical procedure that resulted in an unexpected complication, your petition for an adjustment will almost certainly be denied.

The importance of ensuring consumers understand how much they must pay for a service before they receive it appears in Figure 2.1. Note the high level of agreement on the need for this understanding across both the hospitality and healthcare industries.

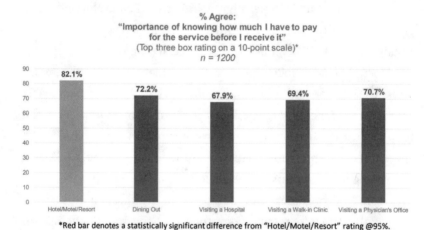

*Red bar denotes a statistically significant difference from "Hotel/Motel/Resort" rating @95%.

Figure 2.1: Importance of knowing the price of a service prior to consumption.

It is precisely the opaque nature of healthcare service pricing that has precipitated a growing crescendo of demand for more transparency. This sentiment is particularly pronounced for services provided in the hospital setting. It was the impetus for the executive order issued by the Trump administration in 2019 (effective January 2021) and continued by the Biden administration.[7] The US Department of Health and Human Services ordered hospitals to publish rates for 300 common medical services such as X-rays, outpatient visits, lab tests, and so on, in an online searchable way. The executive order also stated that hospitals must disclose the payment they are willing to accept for those services if payment is made in cash.

The order is intended to enable patients to shop for lower-priced medical services and reduce their overall healthcare costs. Hospitals that fail to comply face a civil penalty of up to $300 a day. The legality of this order was contested by the American Hospital Association but upheld by the US District Court for the District of Columbia. Industry compliance with the order has been lethargic, however, and none of the 6,000 hospitals subject to the rule had been fined for non-compliance as of January 2022, one year after the order became effective.

As revealed in Figure 2.2, hospitality service providers perform much better than healthcare service providers on pricing transparency. Consumers are more likely to feel the bills they receive from healthcare service providers do not align with their expectations.

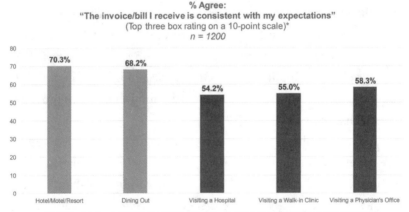

% Agree:
"The invoice/bill I receive is consistent with my expectations"
(Top three box rating on a 10-point scale)*
n = 1200

*Red bar denotes a statistically significant difference from "Hotel/Motel/Resort" rating at 95%.

Figure 2.2: Alignment of service pricing and expectations.

Opacity about the cost of healthcare services, and the corresponding questions and disputes, is presumably the proximate cause for an alarming statistic cited by Dr. Jeffrey Pfeffer in a recent study published by Stanford University: Americans cumulatively spend 12 million hours per week talking to their health insurers, most of the time about coverage and cost.

The collective value of time spent by employed people engaging in these discussions while at work is estimated to be $21.6 billion annually. Lost employee wages for time taken away from work to engage in similar discussions total an additional $26 billion annually.[8] That translates into a lot of phone time. Better clarity about the pricing of healthcare services would clearly be welcomed by patients.

Competition for Patients/Customers/Guests

One of the most significant developments to emerge from the new millennium's "information everywhere" paradigm has been the altered view many sophisticated hospitals and hospital systems now have of the business practices they must embrace to attract and serve new patients. Prior to mass engagement with the internet, hospital systems and most healthcare providers competed for physicians because they were the primary source of new patients through referrals they made and/or received. This has changed with the proliferation of medical symptom-related information online, the omnipresence of self-diagnostic tools, the adoption of more sophisticated marketing practices, and the growing influence of commentary about healthcare providers in social media.

Today, many hospital systems have come to the realization that future patient acquisition will be driven more by direct-to-patient communications as their clientele becomes better informed about options for their care and the related costs. Newly enlightened patients will increasingly sample information and opinions from various sources, both offline and online. They will assess the credibility and personal relevance of this information before deciding which provider they choose to patronize. Naturally, this is subject to access restrictions imposed by their insurance carrier. Hence, most hospitals and hospital systems now compete for patients, not just physicians.

This transformation has led administrators to think differently about how they label and refer to those individuals. Are they patients?

Customers? Guests? The moniker is important because it defines the nature of the relationship between the provider and individual consuming the service. As Dr. Jason A. Wolf of the Beryl Institute so eloquently told us, "There is still a simmering debate about what to call patients."

Consider how the Walt Disney Company addressed this question. Should they refer to individuals who visit their theme parks as "customers" or "guests?" Disney is credited as the first organization to adopt the term *guests* to describe visitors to their theme park in California.[9] According to Savvyhotelier.com, a guest is "a recipient of hospitality, specifically someone staying by invitation at the house of another" while a customer is someone who "buys a product or service." The website further argues, "If you've invited someone to your home, would you do what you can to make them comfortable (i.e., extend your hospitality to them)? I hope so. Would you do that for someone who just wants to buy something from you? Unlikely."[10]

Shoemaker conducted a series of in-depth interviews with patients at the University of Texas MD Anderson Cancer Center (MDACC) to explore this conundrum and posed the following question: "What do you call yourself?" Most respondents associated being a patient with receiving care and establishing a relationship with their healthcare provider. They considered customers to be one-time visitors who purchased a product or service.

Dr. Frederick DeMicco is Executive Director and Professor at the School of Hotel and Restaurant Management at Northern Arizona University. His research interests center on medical tourism, wellness, and the relationship between healthcare and hospitality. Describing the "prepare" stage in healthcare, Dr. DeMicco emphasizes the importance of using system models. He also advocates referring to patients in a novel way: as *patient guests.*

"In hospitality, it is important to deliver a great experience to get top satisfaction scores from guests, build their loyalty and have them talk about the brand in a positive way. Healthcare is no different, because what I call patient guests strongly value how they are treated and how they are afforded courtesy."

When asked how they would like to be characterized, Shoemaker was surprised by their reply. Shoemaker's wife Dr Martha Shoemaker – who helped on the research – discovered that they would like to be treated and referred to as a "loved family member." This term was subsequently used by the Division of Diagnostic Imaging at MDACC to determine the success of different initiatives undertaken to improve the overall patient experience.

Industry Disintermediation

It is evident to even the most casual observer that the "information everywhere" paradigm will soon redefine the traditional business model of healthcare. Physicians will no longer exercise the considerable control they now have over where and by whom patients are treated based on their referrals, as the plethora of information available on the ratings of physicians will enable patients to make more informed decisions about where and from whom to seek care. The ease with which information is now accessed and shared online will facilitate disintermediation of the supplier selection process as healthcare service providers know it today. Once again, an examination of evolved business practices in the hospitality industry reveals some intriguing parallels with implications for the healthcare industry.

Consider the case of travel agents and the conventional role they played in the referral of customers to airlines, hotels, and cruise lines in exchange for a commission earned on the value of those referrals. To improve their anemic profit margin, most major airlines reduced the commission they paid travel agents beginning in 1995. The shoe finally dropped in 2002 when Delta Airlines announced it was eliminating most commission payments to travel agencies after reporting a billion-dollar loss in 2001.

Other major airlines were quick to adopt this cost-cutting measure when they discovered the cost savings they would realize by encouraging consumers to shop and book travel directly on their websites or through a class of distributors called *online travel agencies* or *OTAs* as they are known in the trade. Think Expedia, Travelocity, Priceline, and the like.

Because they do not provide objective opinions or advice on suppliers or destinations or make special arrangements for their clients, OTAs are not travel agencies in the traditional sense. Rather, they serve as a conduit through which industry service providers market their wares directly to consumers, generally at a lower cost. As the audience of online "lookers and bookers" grew, the airline industry's reliance on the use of traditional travel agents to generate new customers dissolved. The number of retail travel agencies declined precipitously as a result. Those that remain in business today pivoted to a fee-based compensation model: they charge clients a fee for making airline and other reservations. Traditional retail travel agencies now play a far less influential role in referring customers to airlines than they did prior to the arrival of OTAs.

A similar transformation occurred in the lodging industry as OTAs began to dominate the distribution of lodging accommodations in the years following the 9/11 tragedy. Their surge in popularity was driven by the confluence of more consumers searching for and making reservations themselves with the resolute belief that they could always find a better deal online. A tsunami of OTA advertising helped promote this claim at the time.

The same transformation is underway in the cruise industry, once insulated by the complexity of itineraries, confusing deck plans, and visa requirements. They are now fully exposed to enlightened consumers who are increasingly comfortable booking directly, both through OTAs and online with the individual cruise lines. This is much to the delight of the cruise lines, although not admitted publicly. They experience significantly reduced acquisition costs through reservations booked online instead of through traditional travel agents, who receive a higher commission. In fact, many in the hospitality industry recall when cruise line executives were roundly chastised by travel agency association executives at industry conferences for the treasonous act of accepting bookings directly from consumers.

Not surprisingly, prescient healthcare executives have taken note of how eliminating intermediaries altered established demand patterns in the hospitality industry. They understand the implications for a more enlightened and efficient path to new patient acquisition. Most major healthcare systems now fund sophisticated online paid search and digital advertising campaigns to reach and qualify prospective patients. Many independent and network healthcare system providers also invest in numerous forms of offline advertising including television, print, and outdoor media for the same purpose.

Yet, as mentioned previously, unlike competition for customers in the hospitality industry, competition for patients in healthcare poses five unique challenges:

1. Ethical considerations govern the composition of marketing messages to ensure they represent the expected outcomes of the promoted services accurately.

2. Regulatory restrictions bear on the composition of marketing messages based on the for-profit or not-for-profit status of the service provider.

3. Legal restrictions impact how healthcare providers may refer patients who receive services paid for by Medicare or Medicaid. They are prohibited from making referrals from which they may derive any financial benefit.

4. Because many healthcare providers are legally required to serve all patients who present in times of need, important profit margin considerations must be borne in mind by healthcare executives when attempting to optimize the mix of patients served.

5. Most healthcare service providers have the added challenge of competing for patients without referencing either the cost or quality of the services they provide, sans third-party awards or quality rankings in media such as the *U.S. News & World Reports*, if earned. Recall the importance of knowing "how much I have to pay for the service before I receive it" from our Gap

Survey results cited previously. Nevertheless, several healthcare service providers have introduced and refined direct-to-patient marketing practices that have enhanced their ability to compete for, and serve, new patients, and at a considerable investment.

According to a report issued by Julia Faria in Statista.com, US hospitals and hospital systems collectively spent $11.6 billion on local advertising in 2021.[11] A 2020 report authored by the American Hospital Association revealed the typical hospital system now spends between one and two percent of its annual operating budget on marketing.[12] Large hospital systems spend significantly more on advertising alone. This allocation has grown as more providers now compete directly for patients. In fact, some healthcare service providers spend upward of 6% of their annual net revenue on marketing, the same level of investment made by many hospitality service providers.

So, we believe the path forward for healthcare service providers seeking growth through the acquisition of new and/or more patients is both clear and inevitable. Direct competition for patients will intensify as information on the cost and performance of providers becomes more readily available and the traditional method of new patient acquisition through physician referrals wanes in importance.

Healthcare executives must therefore become more conversant with marketing methods that reflect how prospective patients seek, receive, evaluate, and act upon the information they use to select healthcare service providers—just as executives in the hospitality industry had to "go to school" on the very same subjects over the past 50 years.

You may be thinking, Well, the hospitality industry is different from the healthcare industry because consumers of hospitality services can stay and/or dine anywhere they like while consumers of healthcare services may only use in-network providers. This is, in part, a fallacy. Although leisure travelers may stay wherever they like, 20% of all trips taken in the US in 2021 were taken by business travelers. This 20% accounted for an estimated 40% of all money spent on travel in 2019.[13]

And not all business travelers may stay or dine wherever they want.

In addition to benefit managers who decide which health insurance plans are available to employees—hence which hospitals and doctors they may see—many businesses, especially large ones, also have travel managers. These managers determine where employees may stay and how much they are allowed to spend for lodging, dining, and so on when traveling on behalf of their company. The parallel to being "in network" is apparent, and hospitality service providers have adapted in order to attract these managed business travelers.

To illustrate the point, consider the following results from our Gap Survey: 69% of respondents took at least one trip for business or a trip that combined business and leisure during the previous year. The majority of them (54.3%) stated the company for whom they worked had specific guidelines on how and where they could consume travel services.

A similar situation impacts healthcare: benefit managers limit the healthcare options available to employees. The physicians and hospitals who provide services for them do not need to compete with all the healthcare providers in the market, just those who cater to employees with certain benefit parameters..

Hospitality service providers have achieved great success at competing for customers, in part, by conducting extensive research to understand consumers' pre-purchase behavior and their post-purchase sentiments. They compare customer wants, needs, desires, and purchase barriers to their resulting satisfaction, willingness to buy the service again, and likelihood of spreading word of mouth (WOM).

Figure 2.3 illustrates the key components of the consumer purchase model. (Note: this model was developed in 1968 by economists. Over time, other academic fields including sociology, psychology, and consumer behavior have created similar models for their disciplines. Our model reflects those designed by economists).[14] Pre-purchase behaviors culminate with a purchase decision, or *moment of truth*, followed by post-purchase behaviors that reflect either satisfaction of dissatisfaction with the purchase.[15]

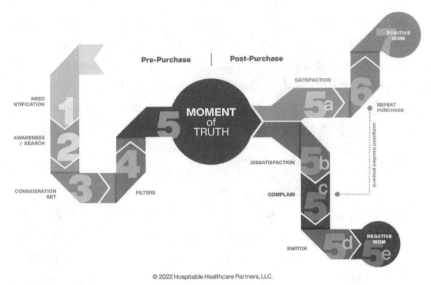

Figure 2.3: Consumer pre- and post-purchase behaviors.

The five components of the model are: *need recognition/problem to be solved/wants; awareness/search process; list of options (consideration set); filters/barriers to purchase; purchase; purchase of the service;* and *outcomes: satisfaction versus dissatisfaction.*

NEED RECOGNITION/PROBLEM TO BE SOLVED/WANTS

The purchase decision normally begins with a recognition or identification of needs, wants, or problems to solve. Oftentimes, this recognition derives from, or is amplified by, exposure to a specific stimulus. This could include, for example, a TV commercial, an online ad, a post from a social media influencer, a comment from a friend, or a direct mail piece sent to a physical or email address.

AWARENESS/SEARCH PROCESS

This is the stage at which consumers begin to search for solutions to their needs, wants, and problems. The search process is dependent upon one's knowledge of the options, however. For example, if someone knows a great deal about the options, they typically search less because they know specifically what they are seeking and, importantly, when they have found it. Similarly, if someone knows very little about the options, they also tend to conduct less search because they have limited knowledge of the options available. Individuals with some knowledge about the options generally search more because they are uncertain about the specifics of what they are seeking and if, in fact, they have found it.

Online search behavior for select hospitality versus healthcare services varies considerably in duration (hours) as revealed in Figure 2.4. The weighted averages reveal an interesting, if not perplexing, observation: Adults spend more time searching for information to plan a vacation (average of 6.85 hours) than to select a physician for a major medical procedure (average of 5.3 hours). This is presumably because of the limited information readily available to consumers about major medical procedures as well as their inability to interpret the information they find. We believe the opaque nature of healthcare service pricing discussed previously also constrains this search behavior.

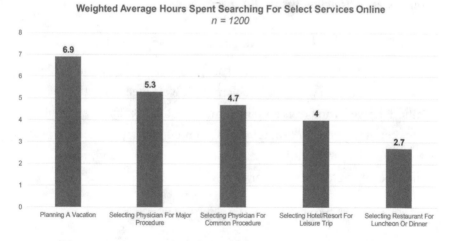

Figure 2.4: Hours spent searching online for various services.

The results of our Gap Survey reveal that social media and brand loyalty also influence search behaviors differently. Consumers consult social media more for hospitality services than healthcare services, and they are more loyal to their favorite hotels, restaurants, and physicians, than they are to hospitals or walk-in clinics. This is an important observation as their loyalty determines which service providers will be considered when selecting a provider for the next procedure. We examine these phenomena later in this book.

LIST OF OPTIONS (CONSIDERATION SET)

Rarely is there only one possible solution to a consumer's need. Often, the consumer evaluates alternative solutions. All possible solutions (typically, brands) make up what is known as the *consideration set,* or the collection of brands from which consumers select one to patronize. The number of brands in the consideration set is dependent on one's knowledge of the category and service options. The less knowledgeable the person, the smaller the consideration set. However, some knowledge enhances the size of the consideration set. Because the service provider chosen is typically part of the consideration set, service providers need to ensure they are part of the consideration set when a search for options commences.

Hotels and resorts attempt to reduce the number of options in the consideration set by encouraging consumers to go directly to their brand website (such as www.hilton.com) to make a reservation instead of going to an OTA site (for example, www.expedia.com) that displays many competing brands. If consumers go to a brand website, they only see the options available from that brand. If they go to an OTA site, they see multiple options from competing brands.

One tactic hospitality service providers use to discourage consumers from looking and booking on OTA sites is to withhold their loyalty program points for reservations booked that way. Another common strategy is to offer bonus points for reservations booked on the brand site.

External information also has a strong impact on provider selection at this stage because consumers have plenty of questions. Does the solution look viable? Is it worth the risk? Is the price-perceived value relationship appropriate? Does the solution address my needs and wants? What is the provider's word of mouth reputation? Is it different or better than that of the other alternatives and, if so, why?

Hospitality service providers undertake considerable research to answer these questions and understand the relative influence of each consideration on consumers' choices of where to stay or dine. We discuss these techniques in chapter six of this book.

FILTERS/BARRIERS TO PURCHASE

Because hospitality services are intangible and may not be evaluated thoroughly prior to purchase, there are certain risks consumers must consider when selecting a service provider. One is the "switching cost" or the opportunity cost of choosing one brand over another. For instance, if an individual is a member of Hilton's loyalty program, they forgo earning loyalty points that would increase their status with Hilton every time they patronize another brand. Hospitality service providers use their loyalty programs very effectively to amplify the opportunity cost of switching brands and increase the purchase dissonance that accompanies acknowledgement that loyalty points have been forfeited.

A second barrier to purchase is the perceived risk associated with the purchase. Consumers might wonder, *What will my friends think of me if I choose this restaurant for our evening out? What if I get ill eating their food? What if the hotel does not live up to its advertised standards?* Some hospitality service providers attempt to reduce the perceived risk of purchase by offering service guarantees such as a promise to address any deficiency quickly and completely, oftentimes refunding the entire cost of the purchase if the guest remains unhappy.

In 1989, Holiday Inn was the first to promote this type of guarantee when it introduced the Hampton Inn brand. Hilton bought the Hampton brand from Holiday Inn and continues to offer a 100% satisfaction guarantee.[16] Premier Inn Hotels, Virgin America, Popeyes Louisiana Kitchen, and Jack in the Box are just a few of the other hospitality service providers who have modeled guarantees after that of Hampton by Hilton.

The prospect of offering a performance guarantee may appear both novel and controversial to healthcare service providers, but not to patients. Consider the case of Geisinger Health System in Pennsylvania, the first healthcare provider in the country to develop and introduce such a program in 2015. As noted by Dr. Greg Burke, Chief Patient Experience Officer of Geisinger, and principal author of the program, the program has undergone several iterations to ensure its appeal to patients and responsibility to the enterprise. Now known as *Proven Experience*, it enjoys the support of both administrators and clinicians, and positive acclaim by patients (more on this in chapter four).[17]

SERVICE PURCHASE

This final risk is where the rubber meets the road. It is where the guest and service provider come together. It is also known as the *moment of truth* because the service is consumed at the same time it is prepared and purchased. As discussed in chapter two, the chef prepares the meal soon after the guest orders it. This is unlike products that are manufactured well in advance of purchase, such as smart phones, where a flaw in production may be fixed before it reaches the customer. This is not the case with services.

5A – 5E. OUTCOMES: SATISFACTION VERSUS DISSATISFACTION

Once a selection has been made and the service has been delivered, what is the outcome? Does performance match, exceed, or fall below expectation? Is the guest satisfied, dissatisfied, or ambivalent? Will they come back? Will they tell others?

The red bars in Figure 2.1 reveal the possible outcomes.

Hospitality service providers undertake extensive research to understand these outcomes and how their customers respond. Do they complain? Do they tell their friends about their visit? Will they return? We consider how hospitality service providers evaluate and understand guests' perceptions of service experiences in chapter six.

A Word About Loyalty

While most of the items listed in Figure 2.1 are self-explanatory, it is important to understand the role of loyalty programs. The hospitality industry uses these very effectively to move consumers through the buying process and create an emotional bond with the host brand. Customer loyalty should not be confused with customer frequency, however. Just because a customer buys a specific brand frequently does not mean they are loyal to that brand. Brand selection is often constrained by availability, not just loyalty. Customer loyalty derives from emotion, while customer frequency simply defines the cadence of purchase behavior.

Patient loyalty will become more important to healthcare service providers as they grow to offer a wider array of services in multiple facilities serving different geographic markets. We discuss the importance of loyalty and loyalty programs in chapter seven.

A New Model: PAEER

Much of the success enjoyed by the most admired hospitality brands is a direct result of their efforts to deconstruct the customer journey into discrete but complementary disciplines, and to maintain a service culture that addresses each. For example, they *prepare* by investing heavily in understanding the purchase patterns, preferences, and profiles of guests. They *anticipate* the specific concerns and desires of guests through ongoing sentiment research. They *engage* guests by creating welcoming environments and ensuring that staff interact with them in a positive and respectful manner. They *evaluate* their performance against specific benchmarks by soliciting and tracking guest feedback about the most critical points of engagement. And they *reward* guests for their patronage to build brand loyalty over time.

These five disciplines coalesce to form a transformational model of service delivery we recommend healthcare service providers adopt to enhance the patient experience: PAEER (pronounced *payer*) representing *Prepare, Anticipate, Engage, Evaluate*, and *Reward*. This model is introduced in Figure 2.5.

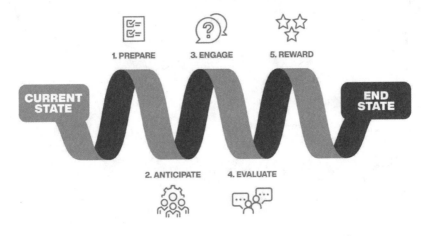

Figure 2.5: The PAEER Model: Five principles of hospitality applied to healthcare.

In the remaining chapters of this book, we introduce this new model in considerable detail. We also demonstrate how hospitality service providers manage and measure each of these principles to enhance the guest experience and create customer loyalty, and we recommend ways healthcare service providers can do the same.

Now, let's explore the first principle in the model: *Prepare.*

CHAPTER 3

Prepare: The *P* in PAEER

"Before anything else, preparation is the key to success."

– ALEXANDER GRAHAM BELL, INVENTOR

Pull Out the Welcome Mat

WE USE BELL'S QUOTATION TO present the first principle of the PAEER model: *Prepare*. It encompasses the administrative steps that should be completed prior to patient visits. Otherwise, administrative detail handicaps the delivery of praiseworthy service upon their arrival.

Successful activation of the PAEER model Prepare principle alone isn't sufficient to enhance the overall patient experience. Rather, health-care service providers must perform each component of PAEER well to achieve this goal. They must think and act holistically, not just focus on one component. For instance, if a provider prepares for the needs of patients well (the *P*) but does not engage them properly during their visit (the first *E*), the overall patient experience will not be enhanced.

However, it begins with Prepare.

In chapter one, we contrasted Roger Conway's visit to a clinic for a colonoscopy with a trip he subsequently took to a resort in Las Vegas. For both services, he made his reservation in advance. Both places of business knew he was coming beforehand. Both presented him with a bill for the services rendered. Yet, his encounter with each could not

James Merlino, MD, the first Chief Clinical Transformation Officer at the Cleveland Clinic, addressed the issue of patient preferences and satisfaction by conducting in-depth patient interviews.

"We thought we knew what patients needed, but through these interviews, discovered what was truly important to them . . . and that we really didn't know what patients wanted. The interviews revealed several important patient needs: communication, respect, service, politeness, teamwork, empathy, and compassion. These conversations prompted the Clinic to create the adage: 'Treat the patient like family; the hospital is your home.'

We developed a plan to excel at delivering on those preferences. Communication was the core. We trained physicians in communication skills with a program that was modeled after the Academy of Communication in Healthcare. Those building blocks were essential to how we got our people to be more empathetic. The training has paid off handsomely for us: we made significant strides in the patient experience and our HCAHPS scores have improved dramatically."

have been more different.

The resort prepared well for Roger's visit. They already knew a great deal about him and made sure the operational procedures required to deliver a welcoming arrival and overall delightful stay were in place. In contrast, the clinic prepared for Roger's visit solely by focusing on operational requirements from their perspective. Many important aspects of Roger's visit related to comfort, concerns, and anxiety were overlooked.

The reason for the difference is the theme of this chapter. We first build the case for why it is important to know as much as possible about the customer prior to his or her visit. We examine ways hospitality service providers—and some healthcare service providers—understand where and how the guest enters into a relationship with the provider and how this familiarity may better facilitate preparation for his or her visit. We then examine how hospitality service providers gather and use this information. Throughout this chapter, we highlight data from our Gap Survey to illustrate prevailing consumer opinions about the importance of service providers preparing for their arrival.

Why Preparation is Important

First, preparation is important because guests say it is important. Preparation rated a 6.79 on a 10-point scale of importance in our Gap Survey. Customers, whether guests or patients, clearly express a desire for all service providers to know more about their preferences. Yet, the five groups of service providers rated in our survey do not perform equally well on this essential aspect of customer engagement, as revealed in Figure 3.1.

It should be noted that physicians' offices rated highest on this variable (54%) followed by hotels and resorts (51%), one of the few variables tested for which the "visiting a physician's office" rating exceeded that of "staying in a hotel/motel/resort." This is presumably because of the personal relationship physicians tend to establish with their patients over repeated visits—evidence of the importance of preparation.

Conversely, restaurant service providers received the lowest rating on this variable (42%), probably because of the high percentage of first time guests hosted by many of these establishments. It would be reasonable to assume a similar explanation applies to the equally low ratings for hospitals and walk-in clinics.

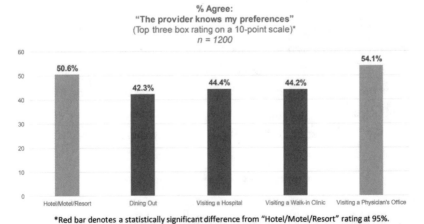

*Red bar denotes a statistically significant difference from "Hotel/Motel/Resort" rating at 95%.

Figure 3.1: Service providers' knowledge of consumer preferences.

Second, preparation is important because of the intangible nature of services. Judgments made about the quality of service are often based upon cues that have no relationship to the actual quality of service delivered. For example, if a check-in line is long and the receptionist does not know a specific guest is coming—even though that guest has a reservation—the stage is set for a negative service experience.

Recall Roger Conway's experience with his colonoscopy. When he checked in, he had to remind the receptionist of why he was there. And a negative experience upon arrival will generally affect the tone of an entire visit. It also impacts perceptions of overall service quality for the same reason. The saying, "You never get a second chance to make a first impression," is clearly true for service providers.

So, what are the best preparation practices maintained by hotels/resorts that healthcare service providers should adopt? There are two broad categories that strive to: (1) expedite the delivery of service; and (2) personalize the delivery of service.

Before examining each, however, we must first acknowledge that healthcare providers serve many patients and may be unable to prepare in a personalized manner because a patient's arrival can be random. It is determined only by the urgency of the contributing medical cause. (Note: the corollary in the hospitality industry is a "walk-in" without a reservation.) In this instance, preparation should focus on the factors that enhance arrival and engagement such as the arrival experience, environmental design, and stakeholder training, which are designed to reduce anxiety. We discuss this in the next chapter when we introduce *Anticipate*, the *A* in the PAEER model. The best opportunity for healthcare service providers, however, is with patients whose arrival is scheduled in advance and for whom they may therefore prepare.

Expedite Service Delivery

To expedite service delivery, it is first important to understand how guests interact with service providers and their employees. It is also important for guests to feel their initial interaction with the service provider is welcoming because it feeds expectations about the rest of the visit. The results of our Gap Survey confirm the significant difference in consumers' perceptions of initial interactions across the five provider categories tested: two-thirds (67%) of respondents felt the arrival experience at hotels/motels/resorts was very welcoming, and significantly more than respondents' sentiments about the arrival experience at physicians' offices (59%), hospitals (55%), and walk-in clinics (55%). Sixty-three percent expressed the same sentiment about the arrival experience at restaurants.

Here are six ways the most successful hospitality service providers prepare for the arrival of their guests.

WAY ONE: JOURNEY MAPPING

Guest journey mapping is a technique hospitality service providers use to understand where and how they interact with guests. Usually, the journey map starts at the time a guest calls or goes online to make a reservation and continues until they depart. The journey map may also be used to investigate subcomponents of the visit, for instance, dining in a restaurant or visiting the spa in a resort. The journey map should detail the specific points of interaction between the guest and the provider to identify opportunities to surprise and delight the guest, as well as potential pain points.

Some healthcare service providers also use patient journey mapping. For example, journey mapping research conducted by Shoemaker at University of Texas MDACC revealed that patients felt they were being treated "like cattle, with no personalization."[1] To improve the check-in process and create a positive first impression for the Division of Diagnostic Imaging at MDACC, the initiatives shown in Table 3.1 and Table 3.2 were implemented:

1	Provide the patient with information necessary to ensure a smooth appointment process (an example of Assurance).
2	Foster a welcoming environment as soon as patient walks into CT 7th Floor-Mays Clinic and emphasize communication between the front desk and the patients (an example of Empathy).
3	Provide patients with the option of obtaining a pager and guarantee the paging system will be accountable and effective (an example of Tangible).
4	Alert the manager of any incidents/complaints.
5	Wear the Anderson Care button and carrying the Anderson Care trifolds (please see end of this chapter for an example of MD Anderson Care) (examples of Tangible and Reliability).
6	Follow the same tactics when talking with a patient over the phone (an examples of Responsiveness, Reliability, Empathy, Assurance).
7	Remember: You are the face of Mays Clinic CT -7TH Floor!!

Table 3.1: Front desk and patient service coordinator goals at MDACC.

1	Utilize the Anderson Care greeting acronym with every patient and caregiver (examples of Empathy, Assurance).
2	Politely educate the patient to respect the privacy line within the new rope barrier system (examples of Empathy and Reliability).
3	Follow the reception area checklist and cover each item on the checklist (examples of Reliability, Assurance, Empathy, Responsiveness).
4	Provide patients and caregivers with the following patient-related documents. The purpose of these documents is to provide more information to improve the patient experience: (examples of Assurance, Responsiveness and Tangibility) a. CT Journey b. While You are Waiting c. After Your Procedure Dining and Transportation Options
5	Utilize the Glitch Report (a form that details service failures) in case of an incident/complaint and email report to the manager. This will prevent the same incident from occurring again (an example of Reliability).
6	Utilize the pager system and ensure proper accounting of the pagers to guarantee their availability during the day. Both the front desk personnel and the nursing staff will oversee making the paging system process successful. To accomplish this, the paging guidelines listed below must be followed: (examples of Reliability, Assurance, Responsiveness). a. When patient requests to leave the waiting area, hand patient a pager b. Record the date, patient's MRN, name and phone number, time out, and given by boxes in the ready call pager log sheet when handing out a pager. c. Ask for the patient's phone number as another way to reach them. d. Inform the patient that when the pager goes off they must return to the front desk with the device. Instruct them that a nurse will take them to the next step of their appointment. e. When the time has come for the patient's appointment, activate the pager to call the patient.

Table 3.2: Front desk and patient service coordinator strategies to achieve goals at MDACC.

WAY TWO: MARKETING RESEARCH

Hospitality service providers gain insight into how guests interact with them through disciplined marketing research, which for most successful providers, includes both *qualitative* (observational and subjective) and *quantitative* (representative sample-based) components. The most successful hospitality service providers replicate their research in accordance with some pre-determined cadence—seasonally if appropriate, otherwise annually—to discern emerging trends in market behavior versus relying on episodic insights.

Examples of the subjects probed by hospitality service providers in this research include: the demography of prospective guests; prevailing attitudes toward specific provider brands; the relative appeal of specific facilities such as on-premise restaurants, exclusive club floors, and fitness centers; the thread count of bed linen, soundproof rooms, and so on; as well as the importance of various services like express check-in/checkout; late checkout; complimentary breakfast, Wi-Fi, and shuttle services; and enhancements to loyalty programs.

WAY THREE: STATISTICAL MODELING

Hospitality service providers also use statistical modeling to help understand how and when guests interact with their organizations. For example, hospitality service providers can easily model how the demand for hotel rooms or restaurant meals can change depending on factors such as price, the weather, and current events in the surrounding area. They can also estimate the times guests are most likely to arrive for check-in. While more hotels and resorts are adding self-service kiosks to expedite check-in, such devices depersonalize the visit and eliminate an important opportunity to enhance the guest experience. The use of statistical models to plan staffing around anticipated demand is therefore gaining popularity.

Healthcare service providers, like hospitality service providers, also deal with issues caused by wait times. In an article published in the *Journal of the American College of Radiology*, Loving et al. (2017), found that out of 3,675 patient feedback reports (both positive and negative), 11.9% of patients commented on wait times and delays. Research undertaken at the University of Texas MDACC revealed that 53.4% of patients found the time between their scheduled appointment and when they first met with a clinician was more than one hour; for 29.7% of patients, the difference was more than 1.5 hours.[2] The research further revealed that wait times were a major reason patients stated they did not have a great experience.[3]

Wait times also have a cascading effect on overall service delivery. When one appointment is late, all subsequent appointments are likely to be delayed as well.

WAY FOUR: PROPER FORECASTING

A forecast is simply a prediction of future demand, typically based on historical data. It is not about shooting for a single number (for example, 80% monthly occupancy in the hotel business) but rather, a point estimate that is associated with a specific level of uncertainty (for example, 95 times out of 100, the actual forecast will fall between x and y). In this way, forecasting is as much an art as it is a science. When prepared properly, demand forecasts may be used to guide more accurate staffing, pricing, and capacity decisions.

Tracking historical data is a critical prerequisite for developing an accurate forecast. Historical data should not only include how many guests or patients arrived on a certain day and time, but also the following information on those arrivals:

- the primary reason for their visit
- the number and composition of people in the visiting party (adults, children, special requirements)
- the expected length of stay

Each of these variables impacts the quality-of-service delivery. For example, a 200-room hotel with one guest per room is operationally quite different from a 200-room hotel with two guests per room. Doubling the number of guests impacts the number of staff needed to deliver satisfactory service at the property's various outlets. A similar corollary applies to the occupancy of hospitals.

Once the appropriate historical data have been identified, forecasting is typically done using stochastic methods. Future demand may be estimated as the average demand for the historical period or as the sum of historical pickup between one day and the day in the future for which you are preparing the estimate.

WAY FIVE: REVENUE MANAGEMENT AND BEHAVIORAL ECONOMICS

A fifth way hospitality service providers prepare for guests is to apply the principles of behavioral economics to shift demand from busy times to less busy times. Research has shown customers will migrate to less busy times if there is an incentive to do so. Usually, this incentive comes in the form of an attractive change in price, often guided through a strategy known as *revenue management*.

The premise underlying revenue management is that prices should vary with demand to maximize the conversion of demand (aka *yield*) at various price points. For example, the higher the demand, the higher the featured price. Conversely, the lower the demand, the lower the featured price. Yield management presumes that each consumer has a different price they are willing to pay based on personal circumstances, resulting in variable demand. American Airlines is widely regarded as the company that introduced this concept to service industries years ago, much to the delight of price-sensitive travelers willing to change their departure day and/or time in exchange for a lower fare.

Robert Crandall, CEO of American Airlines, said at the time, "If I have 2,000 customers on a given route and 400 different prices, then I'm obviously short 1,600 prices."

This statement reflected the fact that the airline discovered it could generate more total revenue by adjusting fares to capitalize on fluctuations in demand than it would by selling all seats at the same price.

The goal of revenue management is to distribute demand by having consumers with a lower tolerance for high prices change their plans to buy when prices are less expensive. In effect, the airline's proposition to the customer was, "Tell us when you would like to depart or arrive, and we will tell you the fare." Conversely, "Tell us how much you would like to pay, and we will tell you when you can depart or arrive and what type of amenities you will receive."

Shoemaker used this approach to help British Airways manage its pricing strategy. This concept is best illustrated by searching the British Airways website for a fare or any hotel website for a nightly rate. Many companies provide different options if the customer's travel plans are flexible. This is why seasonal rates exist in the hotel business and early-bird specials are standard fare in the restaurant business. A recent derivative of revenue management known as *surge pricing* has been embraced by ride-sharing services such as Uber and Lyft whose fares vary throughout the course of a typical day as demand for ridesharing services ebbs and flows.

Given the demonstrated efficacy of revenue management as a catalyst for revenue growth in the hospitality industry, one wonders why healthcare service providers haven't begun to experiment with this technique. It could drive incremental demand for elective procedures and services to less busy times and increase profit. The question is: would it help distribute demand so wait times may be reduced and patients made happier? An equally important question is: would pricing the same procedure differently by time of day, day of week, or week of year yield higher total revenue than maintaining one price regardless of when or by whom the service is consumed?

We believe the answer to both questions is *yes*.

Consider, for example, diagnostic imaging at a major hospital. If pricing is the same regardless of the time the scan is conducted, everyone will want the scan when they deem it most convenient for them.

Therefore, most imaging machines are usually overbooked during the week—causing much patient frustration—but not in use nights or weekends.

There are people who would willingly change the time they schedule a scan in exchange for a more attractive price. Such an arrangement would presumably be of great interest to cost-conscious consumers, self-insured corporations that provide healthcare coverage for employees, and other payors as well. The distribution of demand facilitated by revenue management may also enhance the overall patient experience because shorter lines and a reduction in wait times enables service provider personnel to spend more time with each patient.

Hospitality service providers have embraced the practice of revenue management because it increases yield, or overall margin, over time. For example, one can go to just about any hotel website and see how the nightly rate for different types of accommodations varies by day of the week, based on expected demand. This allows the guest to determine which is most important: arrival day, type of room, or nightly rate, and book accordingly.

WAY SIX: MARKET SEGMENTATION AND PRODUCT DIFFERENTIATION

Hospitality service providers implement the Prepare principle for guests through the strategic use of *market segmentation*, a strategy that assumes the market consists of discrete groups of customers who share a common affinity but whose needs and wants are discernibly different from others. The total market is divided into segments that include people who share common characteristics or preferences—that is, clients who have the same needs or wants or problems to be solved.

Examples from the hospitality industry include guests who prefer upgraded accommodations, to have breakfast included with their nightly rate, to fly first class, or are traveling primarily for leisure versus business. Marketing communications are then crafted specifically to address the known interests and preferences of one or more targeted segments.

Segmentation is important because it helps service providers better understand guests' wants and needs and deliver the specific services that most satisfy them. This knowledge helps them customize the service experience, thereby enhancing guest satisfaction. Adoption of market segmentation has led to the creation of different lodging industry products and services that align with the unique needs of different market segments; a strategy known as *product differentiation*.

Examples include hotels and resorts configured in uniquely different ways such as all-suite hotels, limited-service hotels, convention center hotels, all-inclusive resorts, and so on..

The advent of product standardization in the lodging industry, precipitated by the growth of Holiday Inn, eventually led to the realization that certain types of guests valued specific facilities and services differently. For example, club floor accommodations for business travelers on corporate expense accounts, all-suite hotels that include complimentary breakfast for value-sensitive family travelers, economy lodging properties for budget-conscious travelers, even boutique properties designed to reflect the personality of specific types of guests.

This realization was articulated in a humorous way by Michael Leven, former President and CEO of Holiday Inns. He was fond of saying that when traveling with families, guests of his three-star Holiday Inn properties on Friday and Saturday nights were often guests of four and five-star, more upscale brands such as Hilton and Hyatt when traveling on corporate expense accounts during the week.

Similar innovation has been evident in the restaurant industry. For example, Masterclass.com classifies ten types of restaurants ranging from buffets to fine-dining establishments serving different groups of customers.[4] Not only does price play an important role in these categorizations, but certain formalities, such as how staff and guests dress, the overall interior design ambiance, style of service, ingredient quality, and type of food. Creativity enhances customer satisfaction while fueling the robust growth of both the lodging and restaurant industries. The hospitality industry is now replete with creative examples of both market segmentation and product differentiation—to the delight of most guests.

Prescient healthcare executives have begun to explore the applicability of these same principles to the delivery of their services. Witness the growth of hospitals that now offer upgraded accommodations and services for an additional charge (market segmentation), the increase in the number of hospitals and clinics that specialize in the treatment of only one disease (product differentiation), or the push to make the delivery of care more convenient for patients through the proliferation of walk-in and urgent-care clinics (product differentiation), and a COVID pandemic-fueled phenomenon: the growing number of patients interested in using telemedicine to access care (market segmentation).

Yet, upon examination, the velocity of product and service innovation in the hospitality industry has been much more rapid than in the healthcare industry. Regulatory constraints represent one reason for lower innovation in healthcare, but there are also other, more compelling commercial reasons. The capital cost of introducing new product or service concepts, the lack of pricing transparency, and lower consideration for sophisticated marketing techniques to identify and attract more patronage. We believe that intensified competition among hospitality industry providers has also accelerated the creativity evident in its maturation, a trend now emerging in healthcare as more providers market their services directly to the consumer.

Personalize Service Delivery

One of the hospitality industry's most noteworthy achievements over the past three decades has been its comprehension of customer purchase patterns and how this information is used to prepare for guests' arrival. Hospitality service providers do this because of the highly perishable nature of the services they offer—the revenue potential of an unoccupied hotel or resort room on a given night is lost forever, just as it is for an empty seat in otherwise busy restaurant—and the corresponding need to develop and market services that address those preferences.

For example, Shoemaker stayed at the Beverly Hills Hotel during the summer of 2021. After being welcomed back and seated at a table by the restaurant hostess, the waiter said, "Welcome back, Dr. Shoemaker. You will be happy to know we are making your favorite McCarthy salad again."

The waiter was able to do this because Shoemaker's picture, his preferences, and his past orders were all captured in the hotel's database. They even knew the name of Shoemaker's cat, Ripley. The waiter asked how Ripley was doing before mentioning he was a dog person, and the two had a spirited exchange about the joys and sorrows of pet ownership.

Mr. Edward Mady, former Regional Director of West Coast USA and General Manager of the Beverly Hills Hotel and Hotel Bel-Air—both part of the Dorchester Collection—explained that each restaurant guest interaction has a beginning (the initial greeting from the host or hostess), a middle (everything from taking the food order to presenting the check), and an end (saying goodbye as each person leaves). The key, he explained, is to personalize the interaction and create a shared experience—in Shoemaker's case, the joys of pet ownership—so a relationship is established quickly. This shared experience, and resulting relationship, increases overall guest satisfaction.

Do not for a moment think, *Well, of course a five-star hotel can offer such personalized service, but this could never happen in a less-celebrated operation.* Even hotels that charge less than $120 per night can create shared experiences and relationships.

For example, when Shoemaker checked into a Marriott Residence Inn at the Burlington, Vermont airport, he was greeted with, "Hello Dr. Shoemaker, welcome back to Marriott." The desk clerk further explained, "I know you love an early morning cup of coffee and wanted to let you know we brew coffee here 24 hours a day, so it is always ready when you are."

It was the first time Shoemaker had stayed at this Marriott, so how did the clerk possess this knowledge? Because Shoemaker has stayed at multiple Marriott hotels over time and is a member of the company's loyalty program—a database now populated with his preferences as revealed and tracked during his previous visits across multiple locations.

For both experiences to have occurred, each hotel had to know a lot about Shoemaker. In the pre-computer era of the hospitality industry, this information was captured in a general manager's guest book. This book would typically be found at the front desk or near reservations and was required reading for all front office personnel: desk agents, bellmen, valet attendants, and the like. That way, they knew who was arriving that day and who was in the hotel for a multi-night stay. This guest book was the earliest tool used to profile the preferences of guests; a discipline known in today's digital world as customer relationship management (CRM).

Do not confuse CRM with database marketing, frequent traveler programs, partnerships, or relationship selling. Although some of these may be used to enhance relationships they are not, in of themselves, the basis of relationships. The true sense and purpose of CRM is to establish, build, and maintain customer relationships, which leads to brand loyalty and repeat purchases long after the initial production or consumption process has ended.

Gaining access to customer preference information in the hospitality industry used to be problematic until providers discovered a quid pro quo approach with powerful incentives when a guest signs up for the brand's loyalty program and discloses this information. Examples of incentives include free Wi-Fi or extra reward points for booking reservations on the "brand.com" website, free or discounted branded merchandise, or free food and beverages after accumulating enough reward points for redemption.

One of the reasons many guests of specific hospitality service providers remain loyal is how those providers prepare to address their specific needs. For example, members of the most popular loyalty programs in the lodging business are asked to share preferences in their membership profiles so host properties may accommodate them in advance of their arrival. Examples include the preferred type of bedding, pillows, check-in protocol, and other selections from available amenities. Most also enable guests to alert the host property to any special requirements such as extra bedding or child-care services

Multi-unit hotel chains make this information available to any property in their system, regardless of whether that property is owned, operated, or franchised, so the desired guest experience is replicated with consistency across the brand's entire portfolio of locations.

The airline industry also applies the Prepare principle to frequent travelers. Members of the most popular frequent flyer programs are invited to share their preferences for such things as seat location, boarding sequence, reward miles acquisition, and payment options. Frequent flyers with loyalty status are invited to step out of longer lines when checking in and enjoy first boarding privileges at the gate to ensure access to highly coveted overhead bin space.

Another way hospitality service providers prepare for guests is to study their expressed preferences over repeated points of engagement, such as nights in hotels or meals in restaurants, to reflect evolving customer preferences. These are typically made unobtrusively through data accumulation and manipulation without the direct knowledge of the guest. Individual patrons of Domino's, for example, often marvel at how the team member taking their phone-in order can recite their preferred crust, toppings, and sides without being asked to disclose them. This is enabled by the sophisticated use of CRM.

Casino hotel operators are especially adept at the Prepare principle, going to great pains to understand the nuanced preferences of their most important, high-rolling customers, affectionately referred to as *whales*. They do this by assigning a host to each whale whose role is to address the whale's every need, and those of his or her family—the ultimate expression of preparation.

Another technique practiced by hospitality service providers is to obtain access to administrative information on each guest prior to arrival. This typically includes the latest contact information, preferred contact time and method, confirmation of credit and billing procedures, and other details that can provide service more efficiently. At The Beverly Hills Hotel and Bungalows, this information is kept on a server that can be accessed from a staff member's mobile device to facilitate the arrival process of each guest. Think of this as the traditional General Manager's Book meeting the twenty-first century.

While some guests may think it is creepy for the service provider to have so much personal information, it is important to note that recent privacy laws such as the General Data Protection Regulation (GDPR) in the European Union and the California Consumer Privacy Act (CCPA) in the US provide protections. They allow each guest to determine what type of data may be collected, how it is stored, and provide the opportunity to see and request its deletion.[5]

Successful restaurant operators use frequent diner programs to track the preferences of guests and ensure that their properties offer the dining services and selections their customers will likely want to have. Examples include making sure

Mostafa Boutajrit, VP of Loyalty, Financial Services and Customer Assurance at Caesars Entertainment, joined the company about the same time they launched their legendary loyalty program over 24 years ago. He explained how the company continues to engage customers through this widely admired program.

"When the loyalty program started, it was an earn and burn program (earn rewards and use them). Then we introduced benefits to encourage repeat patronage, such as access to a VIP lounge; then experiences, such as meeting a celebrity; then partnerships, such as discounts on a cruise line. Members responded very positively.

We are a data driven company, so we look at the data. We look at customer behavior. We look at the customer's voice, then we determine the equilibrium where the voice of the customer and data meet. The value proposition from this is huge. If you surprise and delight customers, that creates emotional loyalty."

customers always get their favorite wines, are seated at their favorite tables, are invited to a chef's table in the kitchen, and are offered special items not readily available to others. Restaurant operators also use this information to grant loyal guests' special access to otherwise difficult-to-get reservations on special occasions such as Mother's Day and other popular holidays.

It is important to note that most of these pre-arrival protocols are intended to enhance the convenience of service delivery; the personalization aspect of PAEER ascends in importance at the points of arrival and engagement. This is increasingly important in the bold new service world that operates at the speed of the internet, especially for Millennial and Gen Z customers.

Healthcare providers must access and manage patient information in a manner that conforms with HIPAA (Health Insurance Portability and Accountability Act).[6] However, there is no reason basic profile information can't be captured and used responsibly by providers to facilitate preparation in a similar manner to that practiced by the most successful hospitality service providers. This is particularly true for healthcare service providers who are patronized regularly or repeatedly by the same patients.

Patient healthcare data reside in electronic medical records and, understandably, are curated primarily to guide and facilitate clinical care. The interoperability of this information across different providers and locations is problematic for regulatory, technical, and administrative reasons. However, it is reasonable to assume the addition of non-clinical preference information to patient records would enable providers to prepare for the patient arrival in a more welcoming manner. This could include basic contact information, insurance information, preferred pharmacy, rooming preference for in-patient care, dietary requirements and preferences, religious preference, transportation assistance—even preferred language. And the addition of information that would reduce or eliminate the exhaustive task of filling out the additional and repetitive administrative forms that are often presented at the time of the appointment would enhance the patient experience as well.

The process and cost of gaining the actionable insight necessary to facilitate preparation need not be burdensome. It should, however, be disciplined. Hospitality service providers achieve this through a roster of initiatives that typically includes the following:

- Ongoing environmental scanning that tracks and reveals trends in market consumption patterns and preferences. Yesawich spent many years supervising this type of research as CEO of a prominent marketing services agency serving hospitality industry clients along with publishing an annual report that is widely recognized as the "go to" source on the emerging travel habits, preferences, and intentions of Americans: *The MMGY Global Portrait of American Travelers.*[7]

- Baseline composition with an annual refresh of existing customer profiles to discern consumption patterns, preferences, and emerging issues and opportunities. These profiles typically include information on the demography and geographic origin of existing customers, their consumption patterns, and media habits. More sophisticated profiles include psychographic information and social values.

- Quantitative marketing research (representative, large sample-based) that is conducted so the results may be projected to the population of all similar guests within a defined range of statistical confidence. Quantitative research is frequently supplemented with enlightening observations gleaned through the application of qualitative research (observational and subjective). This is particularly true on topics that are complex and/or about which respondents are either reticent or unable to express their sentiments accurately.

- Qualitative research, either small or convenience-sample based, is frequently used prior to the implementation of quantitative research to provide insights when designing survey instruments. For instance, qualitative research may reveal the reasons someone visits one service provider over another. These reasons may then be defined and prioritized further in a larger quantitative study that enables more insightful statistical analysis. One should not rely solely on qualitative research results to guide important decisions, however, because of the small sample sizes and unstructured nature of engagement. Yet, the resulting insights may be quite provocative. As an example, hospitality service providers have always focused on the arrival experience as an important determinant of guest satisfaction. Obvious contributors include the architecture, layout, interior design, furnishings, lighting, and sound of the arrival space. Qualitative research also revealed that, depending upon the time of day, infusing ambient aromas in public areas evoked different emotional reactions. The same principle applies to ambient music. Healthcare providers should take note of this given the aromas and sounds that pervade the public areas of their facilities. We share additional insights about these techniques in the next chapter.

Although Prepare is the first principle in the PAEER model, it provides the opportunity to exponentially improve overall patient satisfaction through enhancements to the actual arrival experience. This is because of the unique emotional state that often characterizes patients' encounters with healthcare service providers. They may be in pain, fatigued, anxious, uncertain, afraid, or even skeptical about the care they are about to receive. These sentiments lurk below the surface as catalysts for a potentially negative patient experience. Alternatively, anticipating patients' emotions and addressing these emotions through the examples illustrated in this chapter can convert these sentiments into experiences that enhance patient satisfaction.

How to Prepare To Deliver Hospitable Healthcare

In this chapter, we introduced a variety of ways the hospitality industry prepares to serve its guests. Some of these are quite sophisticated, such as using the probability theory to estimate guest arrival times, yet most are relatively easy to implement. Below are four of the most important things that healthcare service providers should implement to enhance the patient experience:

1. Using the patient experience mapping process, identify the specific points of engagement between staff and patients. For each point of interaction, have staff develop tactics to introduce each component of the RATER system (chapter one) to remind patients they are receiving quality service. These could be as simple as creating scripts that detail the words staff should use to communicate with patients or the introduction of an amenity such as a comfort blanket for patients who state they are cold.

2. When conducting patient research, providers shouldn't just focus on operational issues like whether or not a patient was greeted with a smile. Instead, they should ask questions that enable the healthcare team to develop comprehensive patient profiles and determine patient preferences that may be used to enhance their overall experience.

3. Consider the fact that perception is reality. This chapter has illustrated how hospitality service providers have used principles of consumer psychology, behavioral economics, and revenue management to convert unfavorable perceptions into favorable ones. One example showed how the hotel industry gives customers the opportunity to decide which is more important: the nightly room rate or the desired arrival date. The element of choice changes the customer's perception of who is responsible for the outcome. If there is only one choice, responsibility for the

outcome accrues entirely to the service provider. When multiple choices are offered, the customer and the service provider share this responsibility.

4. Invest in the development of a patient CRM program. As stated previously, a CRM program would encourage patients to share with their healthcare service providers their likes and dislikes and other pertinent information, such as any medications they take, from the prescriptions to over-the-counter treatments. The service provider may use this information to determine their behaviors and preferences, and then address them without patients ever having to ask.

CHAPTER 4

Anticipate: The *A* in PAEER

"Our worst fears lie in anticipation."

– DON DRAPER, A CHARACTER PLAYED BY JON HAMM IN THE
TELEVISION SERIES, *MAD MEN*

Arrival Experience

AS WE DISCUSSED IN CHAPTER THREE, the hospitality industry has invested considerable time, energy, and talent to prepare for guest arrivals. Their efforts reflect a deep understanding of guests' predispositions, preferences, and worries, and they offer solid guidance for applying the second principle in the PAEER model: *A* for *Anticipate*. By anticipating guests' needs and concerns, they are better able to ensure guests feel welcome from the moment they arrive.

The same is not always true in the healthcare industry. Let's begin this chapter by comparing common arrival experiences in healthcare and hospitality.

The Waiting Room

As Roger Conway walked through the door of the clinic, he was full of anticipation and anxiety. After all, he had watched several hospital dramas on TV and witnessed the complications that often accompany surgery. So, before he checked in with the receptionist, he wasn't sure if he should be in "fight" or "flight" mode. The uncomfortable chairs, dated magazines, claustrophobic seating area, and hushed conversations he overheard in the waiting room did little to allay his concerns.

Roger settled into a chair and watched the video loop running on the wall monitor. It was sponsored by a pharmaceutical company, broadcasting information of little interest to him in his present state. He also noticed a gurney just inside the door to the clinic which conjured up images of patients in distress being rushed to an awaiting team of masked clinicians. The specter was unsettling to Roger.

Suddenly, the door to the clinic opened and the nurse announced the name of the patient whose time had come: "Richard!" No one in the room responded, so the nurse called out again, this time a bit louder: "Richard!"

Roger watched as all eyes turned to the slight, elderly man who had just realized the nurse was calling him. The man rose and then shuffled through the door to meet his destiny. The other patients bowed their heads once again and resumed their hushed conversations.

Roger dreaded the moment when the nurse would emerge from the door and shout his name for all to hear.

The Lobby

As Roger and his wife walked through the elegant entrance of the Las Vegas resort where they would be staying, Roger was anxious and full of anticipation. After all, they had not taken a relaxing getaway for a long time—she always said he worked too hard—and he wanted to make sure they would have a great time. Again, he defaulted to his usual fight or flight mode.

The first thing he observed upon entering the lobby was the laughter of other guests. He also noticed soothing background music piped throughout the lobby and saw smiling employees welcoming other patrons, helping with their luggage, answering questions, bidding them "good luck" in the casino and, most of all, wishing them an enjoyable stay. Roger also sensed a faint but pleasant aroma in the air.

At the reception desk, he was greeted by name and asked only to present proper identification. While being escorted to their room, Roger and his wife were offered cold towels to freshen up and a complimentary arrival beverage to enjoy. At once, his anxiety turned to excitement, and he thought, *This is going to be a great weekend!*

The Contrast

Both scenarios involved the purchase of a service which, as discussed in chapter one, could be fraught with problems because production and consumption happen simultaneously. This unique service characteristic is why anticipation is fueled by emotions. When buying a product, there is generally an opportunity to kick the tires prior to purchase, so the customer's emotions may be interpreted within the context of the anticipated behavior. This is not the case with the consumption of services, however. Service providers must therefore anticipate and address the emotions of customers to enhance their satisfaction.

The staff at the doctor's office did little to anticipate Roger's emotional state prior to his arrival. From their perspective, Roger's visit began when he entered the clinic. They focused on the administrative and procedural aspects of his visit, paying virtually no regard to his unexpressed anxieties.

The resort in Las Vegas, however, considered Roger's visit to begin when he first visited the resort's website and made his reservation. By implementing the Anticipate principle of the PAEER model, management predicted Roger's emotional state and took several steps to allay any concerns he had prior to his arrival.

In the previous chapter, we examined how hospitality service providers prepare for guests' arrivals (the *P* in the PAEER model). In this chapter, we introduce how hospitality service providers anticipate the concerns harbored by guests prior to their arrival, take specific actions to address them, and suggest how the techniques they have refined may be exported to healthcare to enhance patient satisfaction. First, however, we must understand the unique context within which each type of service is consumed.

What Providers Should Anticipate and Why

Have you ever felt anxious about visiting a doctor? A hospital? Or how about hosting a special occasion meal in a restaurant you have never visited before? Well, that's perfectly normal because we anticipate possible outcomes of such encounters and occasions.

Anticipation is a natural precursor of the consumption of many services, especially those in which we make a significant emotional or financial investment. This is evident when people express how they feel about a special evening out at an expensive restaurant, or a relationship-building weekend away with a spouse or partner at a pricey resort, such as Roger's trip to Las Vegas. It also explains why many individuals are anxious about visiting a healthcare provider: uncertainty about the outcome feeds their anxiety.

Some people also suffer from a generalized fear of doctors at some point in their life. This is known as *iatrophobia* and may cause you to "avoid seeking medical care even when you're very sick because you have extreme anxiety or panic attacks."[1]

This should come as no surprise, given the uncertainty associated with many medical procedures, both simple and complex. The accuracy of the diagnosis, the outcome of the treatment, possible side effects, recovery time and, of course, the cost, can be cause for concern.

Medical fear may also derive from anxiety about specific medical procedures such as blood draws, anesthesia, dental work, or the claustrophobia induced by an MRI scan.

We believe six aspects of healthcare are the primary catalysts of patients' anxiety:

1. the diagnosis;

2. the recommended treatment;

3. possible unknown outcomes of the treatment;

4. the cost of the treatment;

5. the attitude of the staff that delivers the care; and

6. the inconveniences they will likely endure throughout the process like repetitive forms requesting the same information provided on the last visit, wait times for appointments, billing disputes, and so on.

Direct engagement with the clinical team is generally required to address the first three contributors, but much may be done by providers to address the last three. This is where principles and practices refined by hospitality service providers may have the greatest impact on the patient experience.

Progressive healthcare providers have attempted to mitigate the related anxiety through such things as the design of more welcoming arrival environments, pre-registration to minimize the time required to collect and approve administrative information upon arrival, training staff to become more observant and empathetic, the issuance of pre-arrival messaging that includes instructions about what to expect, even the vicarious introduction of clinical teams through the issuance of pre-arrival videos.[2]

Mardelle Shepley, DArch, is Executive Director of the Cornell Institute for Healthy Futures at Cornell University, the first academic center in the country to combine hospitality, environmental design, health policy, and management to improve service in healthcare, wellness, and senior living. Dr. Shepley applies evidence-based research to environmental design.

"Environmental psychology aims to improve the patient experience by giving patients a choice. In medical situations, patients relinquish control and there's a feeling of helplessness. We want to reduce the amount of stress by giving patients choices and control. Examples include good wayfinding and waiting rooms with seating options.

Positive distraction deflects people from focusing on negative experiences, such as waiting. These include views of nature—trees and the outdoors—and access to nature walks, artwork, music, and social interactions with a family member. All these have biological effects on patients."

Hospitality Industry Practices

The most successful hospitality service providers have adopted myriad practices to assuage the anticipated anxiety of guests prior to their arrival. This true for both positive anxiety, say, when planning a weekend away; and negative, say when traveling to a new destination the first time, perhaps one in which a foreign language is spoken, or the currency is different. Most of these entail the collection and use of information and/or communications required to facilitate the visit and/or transaction. Examples from the lodging industry include

- a guarantee of the availability and price of accommodations when booked;

- a guarantee of "last room availability" to ensure you will always get a room, regardless of the hour you arrive and/or occupancy of the facility, especially for guests who are members of the brand or property's loyalty program;

- pre-arrival confirmation of stay preferences such as the room location, type of bedding, pillow selection, expected arrival time, preferred in-room amenities like bottled water, snacks, free Wi-Fi, and delayed check-out;

- remote check-in to bypass reception upon arrival;

- complimentary airport and local area transfers;

- preferred form of payment for services rendered;

- preference with respect to conferral/use of loyalty program points; and

- a pre-arrival welcome message soliciting any requests for special services required during one's stay.

It should be noted that the latest hotel/resort property management systems, or *PMS* in the parlance of hoteliers, are designed to consolidate this information in easy-to-use mobile apps that enable guests to bypass the reception desk upon arrival.

Naturally, much of this information is captured and updated in the guest records populated by members of the host facility's loyalty program. Access to this information enables providers to address the individual preferences of guests and serve them in a more personalized, efficient manner. The resulting impact on guest satisfaction is palpable.

Healthcare service providers could adopt similar techniques to enhance patient satisfaction. Specifically, they could capture most, if not all, of the administrative information required from patients prior to their arrival to minimize the time devoted to these tasks upon arrival. Examples would include addressing and resolving questions about insurance coverage and payment. Importantly, they could also capture the information required to commence development of a database to track patient preferences, thereby facilitating future visits.

Select operational techniques adopted and refined by successful hospitality service providers to enhance the guest arrival experience are presented below and contrasted with the arrival experiences commonplace in healthcare.

PRE-ARRIVAL

Hospitality

- The best hospitality service providers use the time between when guests make a reservation and when they arrive to confirm their reservation and create positive anticipation about what to expect during their stay. An example of this type of communication from the Inn at the Market in Seattle, Washington is shown in Figure 4.1.[3]

Discover Seattle

TOURS   DINING   SPORTS

This reservation is guaranteed for late arrival. In the event the guest does not arrive at the hotel, one night's room and tax will be charged unless the reservation is cancelled 24 hours prior to 4:00 PM day of arrival.

Your credit card is used to guarantee the reservation and has not been charged. Please present credit card at time of check-in. To arrange pre-payment of room, please contact the hotel directly.

To change your reservation, please contact the hotel directly at 1-800-446-4484 and our agents will assist with your reservation changes.

We look forward to serving you,

Figure 4.1: Sample hotel pre-arrival message. Used with permission from The Inn at the Market management.

Healthcare

- Healthcare service providers may send a text or leave a voicemail reminding patients of their scheduled appointment day and time. Additional content, if any, tends to be administrative or procedural in nature: "You should not eat or drink anything other than water after 10:00 p.m. on the evening prior to your visit."

ARRIVAL

Hospitality

The receptionist is usually standing—not sitting—behind the registration desk, makes eye contact with the guest approaching the counter and welcomes the guest by name. For example, the Ritz-Carlton Hotel Company has a 10/5-foot rule: At ten feet, employees are instructed to make eye contact with guests, and at five feet, employees are instructed to smile and say hello to guests, preferably addressing them by name.

All guests are not created equal based on their relative importance to the enterprise (more on this later.) Guests who have achieved preferred status because of their previous patronage are typically greeted in a separate registration area and frequently pre-registered so they may bypass the traditional registration process.

All guests are presented with a registration form that is pre-populated with the information they provided when they made their reservation and/or is part of their loyalty program profile. Thus, they only need to verify the accuracy of this information upon arrival.

Healthcare

- The receptionist is usually seated, often fixated on a computer screen, and may give the arriving patient a cursory glance and welcome, at best.

- Everyone checks in at the same place, regardless of their relationship with the provider, including whether it is a first time or repeat visit, the duration of their relationship with the provider, the frequency of patronage, and so on.

- The patient is typically asked to initial a master sign-in sheet, given a clipboard with multiple forms which they are instructed to complete or update. Many of these forms could have been completed in advance of his or her visit.

- The patient is then instructed to take a seat in a communal waiting area until hearing their name announced by the assistant who emerges from the clinic entry door. Of note: Some healthcare service providers announce numbers rather than names to let patients know when the clinician is ready to see them. Most patients are familiar with this "now-serving-number-x" approach to service delivery—reminiscent of a visit to their local deli.

POST-ARRIVAL

Hospitality

- Guests typically receive a recorded welcome message from property management on their room phone with a request to notify the reception desk if anything appears awry. The recorded message is replaced with a personal phone call from the registration clerk. The most attentive hospitality service providers prefer to speak with the guest directly instead of leaving a voicemail message.

- Loyalty program members frequently find a delightful welcome amenity upon entering their room, such as a complimentary snack or beverage.

- Guests whose accommodations are not ready because of their early arrival time may be offered a voucher for use at one of the property's food and beverage outlets while their room is being prepared. They are subsequently alerted to its availability via a text message when ready.

Healthcare

- The clinician's readiness to see the patient is typically heralded by a shout from a nurse for all in the waiting room to hear. This may be repeated if the patient is engrossed in one of the promotional brochures published by a pharmaceutical sponsor, watching a video loop on the waiting room monitor, or scanning messages on his or her mobile phone.

- Patients are rarely told how long the wait may be before they see their clinician, even though long wait times are frequently mentioned as a primary cause of patient dissatisfaction.

A Performance Guarantee

As mentioned previously, one of the most compelling strategies adopted by hospitality service providers to ease guests' anxiety is to guarantee their satisfaction. Hampton Inn introduced the first 100% satisfaction guarantee as part of its twenty-fifth anniversary in 1989 and articulated the guarantee in a clear and convincing manner: "If you're not 100% satisfied, we don't expect you to pay. That's our promise and your guarantee."

Several lodging companies and at least one popular food delivery organization now offer some form of satisfaction guarantee. For example, the Grubhub guarantee states: "We understand that delivery issues are often due to elements outside of the restaurant's control and can negatively impact a diner's experience and the restaurant's reputation. With our on-time delivery guarantee, diners will receive a Grubhub Perk if an order arrives late."[4]

This promise is operationalized through the empowerment of stakeholders to do whatever is responsible and necessary to address guest complaints satisfactorily. Failing resolution, an appropriate adjustment is made to the guest's bill, no questions asked.

Senior management of Hampton Inn were understandably nervous about the possible consequences of promoting such a bold service promise. Yes, some financial concessions were made across the enterprise as the program matured. Still, the net effect was an increase in market share, incremental systemwide revenue, greater customer loyalty, and higher guest satisfaction. In short, a real win-win.

One wonders if a satisfaction guarantee could apply to certain aspects of healthcare, especially services for which the outcome is generally manageable and quite certain. Clinic wait times, turnaround times for test results, prompt resolution of financial disputes, and the level of empathy displayed by staff are just a few of the opportunities for patient engagement that come to mind.

As mentioned previously, a provocative attempt to guarantee

Greg Burke, MD, FACP, the Chief Patient Experience Officer at Geisinger Health System, an innovative healthcare service provider, explains their unique Proven Experience program which offers patients a "warranty" on the quality of the patient experience:

"It seemed like the right thing to do to both our clinical and administrative teams. If there was a failure in communication, a delay in getting back to you with your results, a long wait in the emergency room and nobody checked to see how you were doing, your room was too cold, the food was late, the nurse was rude, the physician said something that was very hurtful or egregious, or any number of things that would diminish your trust in the experience, we would offer a refund. Patient satisfaction scores climbed during the first five years after inception.

Initially, we were nervous about the program's impact on our finances; yet the program hasn't resulted in a significant financial hit to the organization. And when we looked at the adjustments we made to charges in the years prior, the results were similar to those we made back then. But the program's positive impact on our reputation within the communities we serve has been very rewarding."

performance in healthcare was adopted by the Geisinger Health System in 2014. The initial concept was to guarantee patients that they would not be responsible for copays or any additional charges for select procedures or services that failed to achieve the intended outcome in a manner deemed satisfactory by patients. With the Proven Experience program, the inherent promise to patients is both simple and compelling: "If things go wrong, you will get your money back."

Disputes, of which there have been few, are referred to patient advocates who are empowered to decide if a credit or refund is appropriate and, if so, in what amount. According to Geisinger Health System's Dr. Greg Burke, patients and clinicians alike have responded well to the program. Further, total fees credited or refunded to patients since the inception of the program represent a small fraction of the net fees generated, while the goodwill that has accrued to Geisinger within the community because of the program has been significant.[5]

Anxiety About Access

Scheduling an appointment is the first point of engagement for most patients and, therefore, a common source of anxiety healthcare service providers should anticipate. Respondents in our Gap Survey cited access to lodging (booking a reservation at a hotel/motel/resort) as easiest among the five industry groups tested. Not surprisingly, booking an appointment for a desired time at a hospital or walk-in clinic was cited as more difficult.

Numerous variables must be considered when making a hotel booking. For instance, one must consider the arrival date, location relative to points of interest, nightly rate, rate inclusions, applicable discounts, room type, bedding type, payment method, loyalty program, special needs, etc. Given this complexity, what makes booking a hotel reservation so much easier than a healthcare appointment? It is the reservation systems hospitality service providers have developed to anticipate how guests maneuver through this complexity.

Most hospitality service providers have devoted considerable time and resources to enhance the ease of booking and scheduling principally through proprietary online reservation systems. In fact, most major lodging brands have refined the process to enable reservation confirmation in just two or three clicks. The process is expedited for customers who have established a user profile with the host property or brand. Many hospitality service providers have also programmed options that are served automatically when the requested date and time is unavailable. Perhaps best of all, these reservation systems are accessible 24/7/365, both offline and online, provide immediate confirmation, and do not require endless time "on hold" or the intervention of a customer service agent to confirm the transaction.

Admittedly, the appointment scheduling process in healthcare is more complicated because of restrictions or requirements imposed on access. Whether a provider is "in" or "out" of network is typically the first barrier to be crossed. One's relationship with the service provider, as a new or existing patient, typically follows. Dealing with any applicable insurance represents yet another hurdle. Clarification and/ or confirmation of "all of the above" usually precedes any substantive discussion about the ailment for which the appointment is being requested.

And, as most readers will acknowledge, having reached the penultimate step in scheduling, it's rare to be asked, "When would you like to come in?" Rather, the dialogue goes something like this: "The doctor's next available appointment is (_____)." The date and time offered may not align with your availability, so you are faced with the choice of taking what is offered or sourcing another provider you might be able to see sooner. Most patients opt for the former because they dread the hassle of the latter.

Acknowledging the negative impact this appointment scheduling scenario has on patient satisfaction, and the sense of urgency that frequently accompanies requests for medical appointments, some progressive healthcare service providers have begun to deconstruct appointments. They create sequential touchpoints to truncate the time required to get an appointment: an initial consultation followed by actual clinical intervention. They do so by offering the same or next day appointments for the former and follow-up appointments for the latter. The initial consultation is conducted by a qualified nurse or physician's assistant who addresses the time-consuming administrative requirements and conducts a preliminary examination in order to confirm the need for further intervention by the doctor. If the need for intervention is confirmed, an appointment is scheduled with the appropriate clinical specialist before the patient leaves the office.

Anecdotal evidence suggests this sequential process of responding to patients' anxiety about access enhances patient satisfaction, even if the date of the subsequent visit with the doctor doesn't vary from that originally proposed.

The introduction of telemedicine is also a technology many healthcare providers have adopted to facilitate these initial consultations, which has proven popular with both patients and providers. Teleconsults now account for an estimated 20% of all medical appointments.[6]

Hospitality versus Healthcare Access

There is one very important difference in the way hospitality and healthcare service providers view customers' anxieties about access: hospitality service providers do not believe all customers are created equal. This is not to suggest any form of discrimination based on gender, race, religious beliefs, sexual, or political orientation. Rather, the hospitality industry classifies and serves customers in different ways that reflect their relative financial importance to the enterprise. As a result, the most loyal customers receive the most recognition, best upgrades, and amenities.

Healthcare service providers are acutely aware that although all patients are equal in their human value, they are not created equal in their ability to access healthcare treatments and amenities, due primarily to the type of insurance they have. Yet healthcare service providers are generally reticent to introduce programs reflecting these differences. Naturally, they don't want to risk potentially unfavorable optics, often citing regulatory restrictions as the reason. There are, for example, clear guidelines on how providers may attract and serve patients with a government-sponsored medical plan.

This is particularly true for not-for-profit healthcare service providers. "We serve all patients equally," is certainly a commendable mantra. Yet most patients understand that frequent users, or those who spend more money with service providers, are generally served in a different manner than those who visit less frequently and spend less. But it is important to understand there is a fundamental difference between being "served" and "treated."

How Patients are "Served" versus "Treated"

Served refers to the non-clinical interactions that occur between patients and staff. An example would be how and/or where one is greeted when checking into a provider facility. *Treated* refers to the clinical interaction between the patients and staff. An example would be administering tests initiated to make or confirm a diagnosis.

Most of the difference between the two considerations is in how healthcare providers deliver services that address the needs of different types of patients. This is typically reflected in how convenient it is or isn't to serve them. An example is *concierge medicine,* an on-demand service for which some patients are happy to pay a premium to consult with a doctor. Yet this difference dissolves when treating patients, as all patients must be treated with the same level of clinical expertise and compassion regardless of their relationship status with the provider.

Acknowledging the difference between serving and treating guests has enabled many hospitality service providers to introduce programs that serve disparate cohorts of guests differently, with much success. At their most basic level, these programs are defined by the frequency and/ or value of consumption as found in the silver, gold, and platinum tiers of most hospitality loyalty programs. Guests who have achieved the highest consumption levels in lodging are rewarded for their patronage with access to separate registration areas, upgraded accommodations that are frequently to as the *club floor,* special in-room amenities, and other attractive benefits. Frequent flyers relish their priority check-in lanes, premium seat selection, preferred access to overhead bin space, and bonus frequent flyer miles. Many restaurants hold inventory for the exclusive use of their best customers, whether by location, time, or both. Frequent diners are rewarded with special discounts, priority seating, and complimentary desserts.

This strategy has proven its effectiveness in the hospitality industry. It is understood and accepted by customers who choose the level of service for which they are prepared to pay. Of course, not all hotel guests aspire to an evening on the Club Floor and are perfectly happy to stay in more modest accommodations at a more attractive price. The same applies to paying a premium for the privilege of selecting a specific seat on an airplane in advance of a flight. But frequent travelers who are card-carrying members of most loyalty programs are quick to declare their privileged status when it comes to claiming available perks.

We believe this type of market segmentation, and the creation of programs to reflect it, could be equally effective in healthcare if crafted and administered properly. More on this later.

Except for patients who pay handsomely for concierge medical care, most healthcare providers serve patients with commercial insurance the same way they serve patients with government insurance (Medicare and Medicaid), or those who present with no insurance at all. Granted, the prospect of adopting different service strategies for patients based on their payment method is potentially controversial, precisely because of the optics. Still, such an approach reflects the reality of contemporary healthcare economics. It also addresses a source of angst for both guests and patients and derives from an entirely reasonable tenet: patients should be served in a manner commensurate with their value to the enterprise.

Winston Lord is the former Chief Evangelist of OpenTable, a global online platform that helps diners reserve, review, and recommend restaurants.

"We called it 'surprise and delight.' Someone getting their favorite glass of wine, or getting their favorite table, or the chef coming out and serving their main course. The number one thing in hospitality is to be present in the conversation with the diner; to be focused in the moment on that individual goes a long way. That personal touch is critical to the guest experience in hospitality. What keeps people coming back, and what breeds loyalty, is how you are served."

Once again, we make the distinction between how they are served, not treated. Some in healthcare may declare this notion heretical, but the implications for patient acquisition, retention, and perhaps most importantly, patient satisfaction, are profound.

The Arrival Environment

In chapter one, we introduced the Four Components of Service (Figure 1.5). The component most relevant to the Anticipate component

Dr. Cristobal Young
is Associate Professor
of Sociology at Cornell
University. His work in
consumer-driven healthcare
deconstructs what he
defines as the "halo effect"
of hospitality. He cautions
about how the absence
of clinical outcomes in
the assessment of patient
satisfaction represents an
important deficiency in
patent satisfaction metrics,
however.

*"There are two aspects of
medical care: the technical/
clinical part, which happens
behind the scenes; and the
hospitality part, which is the
front stage. A 'halo effect'—
where providers are rated as
outstanding—results mostly
from the hospitality aspects
of care, not the backstage
aspects of medical quality
and patient safety.*

*Medical success and
patient safety are often
overlooked or excluded
from what should be the
proper assessment of patient
outcomes. Therefore,
satisfaction scores do not
reflect the quality of medical
care. This makes the validity
of patient satisfaction survey
data questionable at best."*

of the PAEER model is the service environment. This is often referred to as the *servicescape*, which is defined by Booms and Bitner, the originators of the model, as: "The environment in which the service is assembled and in which the seller and customer interact, combined with tangible commodities that facilitate performance or communication of the service."[7]

It is important to note that the servicescape does not include the actual interactions between guests and the employees of the organization. Rather, it refers to the environment in which these interactions take place, both internally and externally. As defined by Hooper et al. (2013), the goal of the servicescape is to add an atmosphere that enhances the customer experience and that will affect buyers' behavior during the service encounter.[8]

The servicescape is critical to all service organizations because, as discussed previously, services are intangible. Consumers cannot touch or feel them prior to consumption. Consumers, therefore, seek cues to make a priori judgment about the presumed quality of services. Drs. Cristobal Young and Xinxiang Chen called this the "halo effect" of hospitality in their provocative review of existing literature on the subject. They state that, "Hotel amenities and hospitality become proxies for the less visible medical quality that will most impact a patient's life." They further state: "Hospitals that provide excellent bedside manner, comfort, amenities, convenience, and emotional empathy may be seen as providing robustly excellent treatment and considered great hospitals even if technical medical quality is lacking or unknown."[9]

Financial institutions were one of the first to recognize the importance of informational cues many years ago when banks were built using stone, ornate gates, and imposing cages. These were not used to keep robbers out, but to give customers the impression their money was safe and protected.

Most hospitality service providers have mastered the art of creating a welcoming servicescape. Healthcare service providers, not so much. This is certainly true from a consumer perspective, as revealed in the results of our Gap Survey appearing in Figure 4.2.

Notice the percentage of respondents who agreed with the statement, "The arrival environment is welcoming."

Hotels/motels/resorts and restaurants received a rating of eight or better, significantly higher than the ratings ascribed to visiting a hospital, visiting a walk-in clinic, or visiting a physician's office.

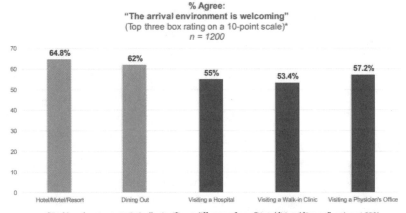

*Red bar denotes a statistically significant difference from "Hotel/Motel/Resort" rating at 95%.

Figure 4.2: Rating of hospitality versus healthcare arrival environments.

Improving the Servicescape

When customers arrive at the physical location of a hospitality service provider, they are immediately impacted by the servicescape, which is the physical environment. The physical environment is broad and includes "anything we can physically experience through our senses: touch, smell, sight, hearing, and/or taste. The physical environment includes both the natural environment and the human-made environment."[10] Thus, the servicescape includes visual design, aromatics, the soundscape, and wayfinding.

Charles White, a Principal of Skyline Art, designs artwork for hospital environments, which differs between patient rooms and public spaces, also among service lines such as women's services, cardiology, and oncology.

"We focus on the health, safety, and welfare aspects of art. We look at cleanability, infection control and the mood of the art in which we create visual interest for patients, families, and employees. We incorporate more soft contemporary art with the use of color instead of hard, cold abstract lines. For example, in orthopedics we create a lot of wonderful custom designs of movement in the imagery with great color and a feel-good aspect. In cardiology and oncology, we create more calming types of imagery."

VISUAL DESIGN

One of the most celebrated hotel designers is Ian Schrager. He co-created and co-founded Studio54 in New York and the Morgans Hotel Group, which includes such hotels as the Hudson in New York City; the Delano in Miami Beach and Las Vegas; and the Mondrian in West Hollywood, New York City, and Miami. Schrager is also credited with the introduction of *lobby socializing*, wherein the lobby is designed to become the primary gathering place for hotel guests and others.[11]

"What Should an Architect Keep in Mind When Designing a Hotel?" an article published in *The Hotelier Academy* discussed six design principles, many of which were originated by Schrager.[12] To help illustrate these points, we have provided three photos, Figures 4.3, 4.4, and 4.5. They capture the lobby of the Ray Hotel in Delray Beach, Florida; the lobby of California's Torrance Memorial Medical Center; and the lobby of Hospitality Hall at the University of Nevada, Las Vegas (UNLV).

Figure 4.3: The Ray Hotel lobby, Delray Beach, Florida. *Used with permission from Gonzalez - Architects.*

Figure 4.4: The Torrance Memorial Medical Center lobby. *Used with permission from Torrance Medical Center.*

Figure 4.5: The lobby of Hospitality Hall, UNLV. *Used with permission from Carpenter, Sellers, Del Gatto Architects.*

What do the photos suggest about each of these enterprises?

Each, in a different way, illustrates some of the six design principles discussed in *The Hotelier Academy,* as summarized below.

1. The Importance of Storytelling

Storytelling in the physical environment reinforces the brand's promise and informs customers of the type of experience they will receive. For example, the large staircase featured in Hospitality Hall (Figure 4.5) suggests that visitors are encouraged to explore the upstairs of the building. Placement of the coffee shop to the left of the staircase lets visitors know those who work in the building are there to serve, otherwise the coffee shop would not have been placed where it could be easily seen and accessible.

2. The Importance of Design Consistency

Connecting the internal and external environments helps soften the transition from the outdoor to indoor space. For example, consider the lobby of Hospitality Hall. Notice how the large clear windows blend the inside with the outside world. The lobby of the Torrance Memorial Medical Center, featured in Figure 4.4, does the same, as illustrated by looking at the far end of the lobby. The Ray Hotel accomplishes this by placing art deco paintings in the lobby, as revealed in Figure 4.3.

3. The First Seven Seconds Matter

The saying, "You never get a second chance to make a first impression," refers not only to one's personal brand, but also the physical environment of service providers. Guests use their five senses to make instant assessments about what the experience will be like. Those who design restaurants use the term LAVA to describe the elements that determine the first impression: Lighting, Air Temperature, Volume, and Ambience.

4. Guest Room Design Reflects Public Spaces

This feature suggests that individual guest rooms must reflect the same level of detail and storytelling as public areas. The lobby sets the expectation for the guest rooms; if the expectation is not met because the guest rooms are not as nice, the impact on the guest experience will likely be negative.

The phrase "private space for the traveler" refers to the fact that the guest room becomes a tranquil place where guests can escape the external environment to find some peace and quiet.

Contrast the typical hotel room with the typical private examination room in a hospital or physician's office. In the latter, there is usually no place to hang one's clothes or even a place to sit, other than on the examination table. The introduction of comfortable furniture, attractive artwork, and thoughtful design would make examination rooms far more welcoming.

5. A Human Design Focus

The space must be designed to reflect how people will use the space. For instance, the lobby should be designed so you can sit alone comfortably if you so desire. Alternatively, should you wish to sit with another person, you can. Or, if you prefer to sit with a group, this is also possible. With COVID protocols in place, buildings are also now being designed and/or reconfigured to provide proper social distancing.

6. Common Areas are Comfortable

The common area in a hotel is the lobby. In a healthcare facility, it is the clinic waiting area. In a home, the common area is the living room. Common areas should be designed in such a way that guests feel they are an visiting an extension of their host's home. For example, consider once again the picture of the lobby of Hospitality Hall (Figure 4.5). Notice the different seating configurations. There are seats for individuals, seats for people to sit together, and seats where groups of people can congregate. In addition, each seating area offers a place for guests to put their things, such as a coffee table, suggesting this behavior is welcomed. Notice also how there is ample space between the different seating areas, thereby providing a sense of privacy.

Color is an important aspect of visual design, and there is a considerable body of literature on how ambient color impacts mood. One firm that focuses on the use of color in hospitality design is Fohlio.[13] A second firm, Simexa, provides a summary of how different colors are typically used when designing hospitality service provider spaces.[14] For example, yellow is used in breakfast areas because it is associated with warmth, optimism, and cheerfulness. Simexa asserts that yellow also promotes happiness and can increase one's metabolism and energy. Shades of green are frequently used in guest room and public area corridors because of their association with stability, balance, and equilibrium. Blue is recommended for bedrooms and spas, as it is typically associated with serenity. Blue is also thought to lower one's blood pressure and heart rate. Red is recommended for many restaurants, as it is believed to stimulate emotions, energy, and appetite. Orange is also believed to be an appetite stimulant. Green is recommended for spas, patios, and outside spaces as it is the color most closely associated with nature. It has been shown to enhance feelings of serenity, tranquility, and health, and is considered an appropriate color for concentration and relaxation. And purple is frequently used in lobby designs because of its association with elegance and luxury.

Figure 4.6, provides an overview of the different moods elicited by various colors and how certain brands are associated with these colors.

Figure 4.6: Sentiments associated with various colors.

Like color, lighting is an important element of visual design. An article in the magazine Mental Floss highlighted research on how lighting plays a huge role in emotional response.[15] With that idea in mind, many hotels have a mechanism to turn on the guest room lights as guests open their doors so they do not walk into a cold, dark room. Hotels in Japan use warm lighting in the hallways every morning to reflect the beginning of the day and cooler lighting in the evening to reflect twilight. Natural light has been demonstrated to affect one's circadian rhythm and may even help reduce symptoms of depression.[16]

Delos, a firm that focuses on wellness through environmental design, created the Stay Well suite which, among other things, provides energizing light to help guests begin their days full of vim and vigor, as well as lighting that helps induce the natural melatonin in the body so one can fall asleep easier.[17]

One healthcare facility that has received critical acclaim for recognizing how environmental design factors influence the patient experience is the new Nancy Friend Pritzker Psychiatry Building at the University of California, San Francisco (UCSF). Opened in March 2022, this 175,000-quare foot facility reflects contemporary principles of design known to enhance the patient experience. Given the highly personal and oftentimes fragile nature of patients being served, special attention was paid to these principles by both the clinical and architectural teams.

Illustrations of the facility's main lobby and pediatric psychiatry reception area are provided in Figures 4.7 and 4.8, respectively.

Figure 4.7: Nancy Friend Pritzker Building at UCSF, main lobby. *Used with permission from University of California, San Francisco.*

Figure 4.8: Nancy Friend Pritzker Building at UCSF, child psychiatry department lobby. *Used with permission from University of California, San Francisco.*

AROMATICS

Scent branding, as it is known, is another important servicescape element. A unique scent may be associated in one's memory with a specific event or product. The diagram in Figure 4.9 illustrates how neurologists believe scent passes directly to the part of the brain that processes emotions and memory.[18] To test this, close your eyes and think about the smell of freshly baked bread or homemade cookies. What images come to mind? Probably some related to home and family. This, of course, is a well-known trick of real estate agents who stage properties for tours by prospective buyers. A special aroma such as freshly baked cookies wafting from the kitchen creates an environment that makes prospects feel like they are touring a home, not just a house.

A 2018 article in *Harvard Business Review* revealed how scented environments have been shown to increase office productivity and reduce errors, increase time spent in a retail store, and get customers to pay more for a product.[19] In addition, research undertaken by Zemke and Shoemaker found that a pleasant scent also increased the number of interactions strangers had with each other.[20]

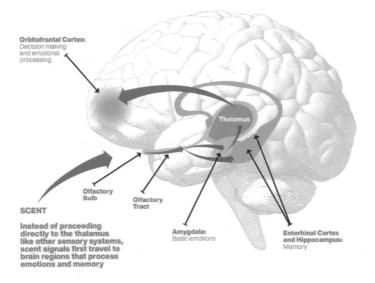

Figure 4.9: The impact of scent on emotion. *Adapted with permission from Marta Zaraska.*

Mirjana Munetic, Associate Principal, ZGF Architects, LLP, was part of the team that designed the new Nancy Friend Pritzker Psychiatry Building.

"Openness to the community and transparency in how the building will operate was a primary design driver at UCSF. Both are emphasized through the central atrium and the materials palette. The five-story atrium is the heart of the building where one can see multiple floors all at once. It provides a frame of reference for general orientation, organizes the program, and supports the patient experience with wayfinding.

Contrary to the harsh lighting and hidden-from-sight approach to traditional behavioral health facilities, the Nancy Friend building uses extensive daylighting, integrated graphics, color, texture, and natural materials. Daylight filters through the skylight baffles, penetrating all the way to the ground floor. Electric lighting grazes the surfaces from the room's perimeter, rather than appearing to come from a direct source, providing ambient light."

Many hotels use signature scents to promote a sense of relaxation in public spaces. One of the first to adopt scent branding was Westin Hotels & Resorts, now part of Marriott International. Their corporate scent is a blend of white tea, vanilla, and wood cedar. W Hotels, also part of Marriott International, offer a scent of lemon blossoms, laurel, and green tea.[21] Sofitel uses Essence de Sofitel, a fragrance developed by famous French "nose" Lucien Ferrero. It's a mix of lemon leaf, bergamot, and basil, supported by lily of the valley, white rose, and cardamom, with a complex bottom note of precious woods like white sandalwood.

Scent branding has also been adopted by more affordably priced hotel brands. Hyatt Place, for example, uses a blend of fresh blueberries and light florals on a base of warm vanilla and musk. Hilton Hotels use a blended scent of white tea and thyme. And the Holiday Inn Express scent—*yes,* even Holiday Inn Express has a scent—is described as "crisp lemon top notes accenting a heart of watery green florals, sweetgrass, a dash of exotic herbs, spicy perilla, and a base of sheer woods and musk."[22] The new celebrity-owned Good Time Hotel in South Beach, Miami, features a fragrance called "Strawberry Moon," which, according to creator Bryan Edwards of Snif, "is for anyone looking for a good time—for poolside, or a day at the beach, a night out—it's good time in a bottle."[23]

Now, contrast the ambient scent in any of these hotels with the scent that prevails in many healthcare facilities. We can surmise that most readers agree: there is considerable room for improvement with the latter.

It's encouraging to note that some healthcare service providers now use scents to help enhance the patient experience, although the practice is still quite rare. For example, in a promotional piece by Air-Scent International, the company discusses how the emergency room at Vanderbilt University's Medical Center in Nashville uses a mixture of vanilla and lavender to calm patients. The piece quotes a nurse as follows:

The goal of the ER's Wellness Committee was to create a healthier environment with increased energy and decreased stress for emergency room staff and to minimize foul odors throughout the department. They tested various essential oils to improve the smells for the entire workplace. We wanted essential oils that would help decrease stress and increase energy.[24]

SOUNDSCAPE

Sounds, like scent, can also have a major impact on one's emotional state. Specific melodies or songs tied to one's memory. To illustrate this point, close your eyes and think about your favorite song. It's likely

Mirjana Munetic CONT.

"The resulting softness combined with the use of the natural material palette establishes a calming and optimistic environment.

ZGF designed separate floors to address the unique needs of the different patients served: children, families, and adults. Examples of this are atrium waiting areas, which have been designed to accommodate different ages and mobilities. There are furniture groupings for young children, taller ottomans and banquettes for older children and adults, and high-backed seating alcoves for patients seeking more privacy.

Each floor features an identifiable color scheme to help with orientation and wayfinding. The result is a complex and rich color palette with textured and smooth surfaces, making the environment feel more familiar and less intimidating.

'The building should not feel like an institution' is something we've heard repeatedly from the client and user groups."

Laurence Minsky is
Associate Professor
of Communication
at Columbia College,
Chicago. His broad
experience as a creative
director and writer
includes the creation of
marketing communication
solutions for companies
such as AT&T Wireless,
MTV, and Nike.
He underscores the
significance of using
ambient scent.

*"Using scent, a company
can communicate a
unique personality for
its brand and generate
positive and memorable
experiences. Hospitals
should take advantage of
scent branding to craft
comforting environments
that transmit a sense of
warmth and caring.*

*Scents, sounds, and visual
elements combine to
create a total experience.
Companies should not look
at one stimulus without
the others since sense-
based experiences are key
when it comes to brand
differentiation. They make
brands unique."*

you associate a pleasant memory with it.

Many hospitality service providers use ambient music to set the mood in public spaces. Examples include classical music played during Sunday brunch, rock music played in bars, and easy listening music to create a relaxing background soundscape in upscale restaurants. For example, W Hotels created its own record label, "W Records," as they believe, "Every Scene has a Soundtrack."[25]

Starbucks has used music to enhance its retail store experience since its founding. The brand has its own profile on Spotify and playlist on the Starbucks App.[26]

Kimpton Hotels has a director of music and brand activation responsible for creating 140 distinct musical identities across the Kimpton lodging and dining portfolio.

Lauren Bucherie, the director, states that, "Music brings people together. It makes guests feel more connected to the location and their experience."[27]

Bucherie believes that service brands should approach music curation in the same way they approach design: by keeping in mind the customer and the emotions the space is attempting to elicit or enhance. For example, the music playing in the lobby during breakfast should be different from what guests hear over a glass of wine in the afternoon. Kimpton Hotels currently have 116 playlists on Spotify.

And there is empirical evidence that reveals the impact of ambient music on customer sentiment in multiple cultures. According to a global survey of 11,255 adults (1,186 from the US) conducted by MarketCharts.com, the majority of respondents agreed with the following statements:[28]

- Music in stores lifts mood (81%).
- Waiting in line was less painful when music was playing (77%).
- Music helps consumers relate and connect to the brand (70%).

WAYFINDING

Wayfinding is also a very important part of the servicescape. It includes all the ways people orient themselves in a physical space and navigate from place-to-place. This is especially true when patients visit hospitals. As evidenced by a provocative insight revealed in research conducted by consultancy Deloitte Digital: 85% of new patients ask for directions when visiting hospitals.[29]

According to environmental psychologist Romedi Passini, wayfinding includes signage, graphic and audible communication, visual clues, tactile elements, and other provisions for special-needs users. Of course, the Walt Disney Company is a master when it comes to making it easy for guests to find their way around their massive theme parks. All who have visited one can attest to this.

The basic rules of wayfinding, as defined by Encompass, and used by Disney and others, include the following:[30]

Identify Landmarks

Landmarks have been used for wayfinding since people have been traveling. Natural landmarks include the sun, the stars, or physical structures such as mountains. At Disneyland, the major landmark is the Matterhorn. For hotels, the landmark is usually the front desk located in the main lobby.

Create Pathways

Perhaps the most famous pathway is the Yellow Brick Road, which Dorothy used to find the Wizard of Oz. Resorts World Las Vegas embraces this concept by varying the color of carpeting and walls to distinguish between the three Hilton Brands located on the property: Las Vegas Hilton, Crockfords Las Vegas, and Conrad Las Vegas. This simple approach to wayfinding makes it easy for guests to make their way through what otherwise would be a very challenging maze of sights, sounds, and places within the resort.

Include Signage at Decision Points

Although this rule seems obvious, signage is often developed by architects who are familiar with the building layout and often doesn't address consumers who must find their way around.

Computer user guides written by computer scientists provide a good analogy. When end-users try to follow the directions, many become lost.

The most successful hospitality service providers avoid this confusion. When they begin the process of designing hotels, they enlist the participation of guests and ask them how they would navigate the property. One hotel casino gave guests baseball caps to wear when they entered. The casino used cameras to monitor where guests went, where they stopped and looked around, and where they stopped to ask for directions. These areas then became signposts in their wayfinding program.

Make Navigating Intuitive

Usually, there are many ways to get to a specific location in a building. If you have ever found yourself looking at a sign like the one in Figure 4.10 below where both ways lead to the same place, you understand how signage can sometimes be completely non-intuitive.

© 2022 Hospitable Healthcare Partners, LLC.

Figure 4.10: Confusing signage.

Make Signage Make Sense

Signage should be durable, colorful, attractive and, most importantly, easy to read. We recommend conducting focus groups with representative customers before signage is created to ensure the messages conveyed by the signage are easily understood by the individuals for whom the signage is intended.

How to Anticipate Patients' Needs to Deliver Hospitable Healthcare.

We began this chapter with a quotation from the TV show, *Mad Men*, wherein Don Draper, played by Jon Hamm, stated, "Our worst fears lie in anticipation." This is particularly true in healthcare because it is easy to imagine the multiple maladies one might have that could negatively affect one's well-being. The fears associated with the purchase of hospitality services are clearly less ominous, but the fear of wasting time and money or having a terrible experience is very discomforting for many guests.

The travel company, Thompson Travel, in the United Kingdom, part of TUI, once ran an advertisement with the following headline: "For just one afternoon in the sun, you spend three weeks and two days working. Your time away is just too precious." The goal of the advertisement, of course, was to encourage consumers to travel only with Thompson Travel, as only they could ensure a successful vacation.

In this chapter, we discussed how service providers may address customer anticipation in a similar way, both prior to arrival and when they first interact with the provider. Below are the four most important actions healthcare service providers should implement to anticipate patients' expectations and anxieties and enhance their overall experience:

1. Issue a pre-arrival pro forma estimate of the cost of the services to be provided, including the portion for which payment is expected from the payor versus the patient. Be sure to include all financial costs associated with the procedure, not just those of the main service provider. For example, in the case of a visit to the clinic that also includes outside tests and/or other services, make sure these are part of the estimate.

2. Issue pre-arrival confirmation of the appointment, including administrative forms that may be completed in advance and include "need to know" information. This will facilitate the check-in process upon arrival and pre-empt the "Do they know I am coming and who I am?" question contemplated by patients, oftentimes with considerable anxiety.

3. Create and maintain a welcoming arrival environment. As discussed in this chapter, the servicescape helps make the service experience tangible. Consider walking into a clinic where the waiting room has white walls adorned with promotional displays from pharmaceutical companies, a TV monitor running looped videos of little relevance, and chairs positioned uncomfortably close to each other. Now contrast that image with examples

of the reception areas shown in Figures 4.3, 4.4, 4.5, 4.7, and 4.8. Which of these arrival environments is more likely to lead you to conclude that you made the right decision about your destination? Clearly, the latter.

4. Introduce separate reception and registration areas for new versus returning patients and modify reception protocols accordingly. This is a very simple but effective way of serving select groups of patients differently and thanking repeat patients for their continued patronage and support.

CHAPTER 5

Engage: The First *E* in PAEER

"People will forget what you said. They will forget what you did. But they will never forget how you made them feel."

– MAYA ANGELOU, AMERICAN POET

Create Memorable, Positive Experiences

ONCE THE POSSIBLE ANXIETIES OF the patient have been anticipated and the patient has arrived, the next PAEER principle to address is *E* for *Engage*—the way service provider representatives engage with patients through customer-centric systems and procedures. The resulting "patient experience" is widely defined as: "the sum of all interactions, shaped by an organization's culture, that influence patient perceptions across the continuum of care."[1]

Although the patient experience begins before the patient arrives for the desired or required care, the essence of the experience derives from the interactions they have at the point of initial engagement with the healthcare service provider.

As we mentioned previously, in hospitality, the points of engagement between guests and employees are commonly referred to as *moments of truth*. During these encounters, service providers meet, exceed, or fail to achieve guests' expectations. At the same time, providers have an opportunity to remind guests about the quality of the service they are receiving. Context is very important, however. As our protagonist, Roger Conway, discovered, the hospital where he checked in for his colonoscopy and the Las Vegas resort where he checked in for a vacation offered quite different moments of truth.

We'll start by exploring the "moment of truth" concept and how it has evolved over time. After a discussion about the strategies and tactics hospitality firms use to ensure positive moments of truth, we'll provide examples of how some healthcare organizations have done the same. Data from our Gap Survey illustrate opportunities for healthcare service providers translate moments of truth into positive experiences for patients. We also show how the different frameworks discussed in previous chapters—such as the Four Components of Service (Figure 1.5) and Gap Model of Service Quality (Figure 1.6)—may yield positive moments of truth.

Moments of Truth

This phrase was first introduced in 1987 by Jan Carlson, then president and CEO of Scandinavian Airlines System (SAS), when he published his book, *Moments of Truth.*[2] The book focused on what happens when a guest interacts with an employee of any organization. Over time there have been several adaptations of this phrase, as detailed in an article in *Forbes* magazine.[3] For example, in 2005 the Chairman and CEO of Proctor & Gamble developed three moments of truth. The first moment of truth (FMOT) was thought to occur when a customer evaluated a product or service; the second moment of truth (MOT) was when a customer bought the product or service;

Michael Leven's guidance on how to discover important moments of truth has been embraced by the most admired hospitality service providers. This was evident in his celebrated stewardship of some of the industry's leading brands including Holiday Inn Hotels & Resorts (now Holiday Corporation) and the iconic Las Vegas Sands Hotel and Casino.

"The single most important thing you can do to improve customer service is become a customer yourself: experience the product or service just like a typical customer. Too many executives don't do this. Not surprisingly, their properties and brands rarely make it to the 'best of' lists . . . yet they seem puzzled as to why."

and the third was when a customer provided feedback on the product or service (FBMOT) purchased.

Google christened a zero moment of truth (ZMOT), which it posited occurred when customers were researching information about a product or service. Finally, an event-driven marketing company called Eventricity Ltd. introduced an intriguing prequel: the less than zero moment of truth (<ZMOT), which was thought to occur when something happens in a person's life that forces them to look for a product or service.[4]

The first MOT for Roger Conway's colonoscopy was his annual physical. For his visit to Las Vegas, the second ZMOT came when he realized his work-life imbalance required adjustment, and that he needed more quality time with his spouse.

Insights from the Gap Survey

Our Gap Survey revealed that, with few exceptions, hospitality service providers meet customer expectations at moments of truth better than healthcare service providers. Consider, for example, the check-in process. As reflected in Figure 5.1, the check-in process at hospitality service providers is considered easy, as compared to the check-in process at both hospitals and walk-in clinics. It is interesting to note the check-in process at physicians' offices is considered just as easy as that at hospitality service providers, however.

Gérard van Grinsven is the former CEO of Cancer Treatment Centers of America Global, Inc. and CEO/founder of The van Grinsven Hospitality Group, a consultancy that creates patient-centered hospitality models for healthcare service providers.

"It is important for patients to perceive staff members care about their unexpressed wishes and desires. Several studies, as well as my own work, have shown the impact of patient satisfaction not only on HCAHPS scores and staff turnover, but also on the length of time patients stay in the hospital. In a truly caring service culture, patients heal faster, and their length of stay decreases."

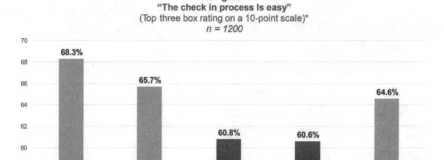

Figure 5.1: Ease of the check-in process.

One possible explanation for patients' more positive assessment of the check-in process at physicians' offices is the attitude of the staff who greet them, as reflected in patients' response to this statement: "The people I interact with make me feel welcomed." It should be noted that although consumers' assessment of this welcoming is still significantly lower than observed for hospitality service providers, it is higher than for the other healthcare service providers as revealed in Figure 5.2.

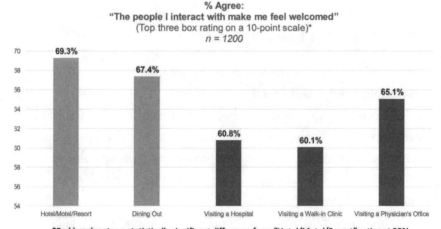

Figure 5.2: Interaction with staff and sense of welcome.

So, how have hospitality service providers been able to achieve such enviable scores relative to healthcare service providers? Because most have developed specific strategies and tactics to ensure positive moments of truth. We discuss some of the most noteworthy next.

Examples from the Hospitality Industry

FOURTEEN KEY WORDS

Edward Mady, former West Coast Regional Director for the Dorchester Collection and General Manager of The Beverly Hills Hotel, teaches his team members 14 key words that mark guests' expectations for service: *Remember me, recognize me, anticipate my needs, give me what I want on time.*

He further explains that every moment of truth has a beginning, middle, and end. The beginning is the warmup, an opportunity for employees to use the guest's name or some other personal acknowledgement such as eye contact or a smile. The middle is the point at which the employee acts upon the guest's request. The end is when the employee bids the guest farewell and encourages him or her to let the staff know if they have questions or concerns prior to departure.

The impact this simple rule has had on guest satisfaction at Mady's hotel is palpable: based on 1,476 reviews on TripAdvisor, the majority of guests rated The Beverly Hills Hotel five stars on cleanliness

Dr. Jason Wolf, President & CEO of The Beryl Institute, is a recognized expert on patient experience improvement, organization culture and change, and sustaining high performance in healthcare. He is a recognized leader of the global patient experience movement and Founding Editor of the *Patient Experience Journal.*

"There is still a simmering debate about whether patients are "consumers." Regardless of the descriptor, healthcare is a business grounded in the idea of human beings caring for human beings . . . and its work takes place at some of the most vulnerable times of peoples' lives."

Edward Mady, Board Member for Surf Air Mobility, and former West Coast Regional Director for the Dorchester Collection and General Manager of The Beverly Hills Hotel, spent two decades with The Ritz-Carlton Hotel Company where he played a pivotal role in the company's successful pursuit of two Malcolm Baldrige National Quality Awards. He subsequently created the Acuity Method, which reflects the desired relationship between culture, customers, strategy, leadership, and the employee team, and defines the path to success for highly performing organizational cultures.

"Many team members who have reported to me have been with their organizations for many years. My philosophy really is not to hire people, but to select them—a vitally important distinction. As leaders we make sure to on-board them properly. We also make sure they understand the real purpose of why they're on a team. They understand what we believe in and understand the customer relationship piece. The promise I make to each employee who joins one of my teams is they're going to grow. We want to add value to their life, and for them to add value to a business. That is the ideal approach in a healthy organizational culture."

and service (reviews collected as of 12/05/2021).[5] And in 2017, Edward Mady's leadership style and commitment to delivering memorable moments of truth for guests earned him the title of "Independent Hotelier of the World" by *Hotels* magazine.

THE HAPPIEST PLACE ON EARTH

In 2021, *Travel + Leisure* published an article that listed the top ten amusement parks and attractions in the United States.[6] Disney properties held four of the top ten listings as follows:

#1. Magic Kingdom Park
   Orlando, Florida

#3. Disney's Animal Kingdom
   Orlando, Florida

#7. Disneyland Park
   Anaheim, California

#8. Disney's Hollywood Studios
   Orlando, Florida

To receive such accolades, Disney must be serving guests in a manner worthy of note and applause. According to the website https://27gen. com/2014/12/15/7-guest-service-guidelines-old-school-disney-at-its-best/, Disney's enviable service standards have evolved over time, however. At one point, staff adherence to the standards was aided by references to the Seven Dwarfs:[7]

1. Be Happy; make eye contact and smile!
2. Be like Sneezy; greet and welcome each and every guest. Spread the spirit of hospitality . . . it's contagious!
3. Don't be Bashful; seek out guest contact.
4. Be like Doc; provide immediate service recovery.
5. Don't be Grumpy; always display appropriate body language at all times.
6. Be like Sleepy; create DREAMS and preserve the "MAGICAL" guest experience.
7. Don't be Dopey; thank each and every guest!

The website further explains that because the seven service standards were hard to remember, Disney management synthesized these into four key points with specific guidelines for each:

Safety

- Practice safe behaviors in everything you do.
- Take action to always put safety first.
- Speak up to ensure the safety of others.

Courtesy

- Project a positive image and energy.
- Be courteous and respectful to guests of all ages.
- Go above and beyond to exceed guest expectations.

Show

- Stay in character and perform your role in the show.
- Ensure your area is show-ready at all times.

Efficiency

- Perform your role efficiently so guests get the most out of their visit.
- Use time and resources wisely. Look at everything through the eyes

Shruti Buckley is Senior Vice President and Global Brand Head, Hampton by Hilton. She is responsible for overall brand strategy which includes driving brand growth and development, diversifying and increasing revenue, and sustaining customer loyalty.

"Hampton's 100% Satisfaction Guarantee has achieved a 20% premium on the average nightly rate compared to direct competitors. It is centered on the little things that make a big difference to guests. It is about making meaningful connections with people in ways that might seem insignificant but really enhance the service experience. It brings humanity to travel.

When people travel, their life is being disrupted so they want to make sure they have a hassle-free stay. Our 100% Hampton Guarantee program is designed to provide just that because guests are more likely to come back if they have a great experience."

of the guest and see how you can make things easier for the guest.

- DisneyAtWork.com describes approaches to efficiency as looking for ways to reduce lines and hassles, providing accurate and timely information, being knowledgeable about your service area and beyond, and sharing opportunities to improve your area.

HAMPTON INN BY HILTON[8]

As mentioned in chapter two, Hampton Inn by Hilton was the first lodging company to offer a 100% satisfaction guarantee. This is known as the Hampton® Guarantee™. After extensive research with customers and owners, however, the brand felt the initial guarantee focused too much on the physical aspects of the stay and not enough on the emotional components. To address this deficiency, the brand embarked on an effort to create a distinctive service culture known as Hamptonality™. The culture focuses the attention of employees—known as "team members"—on delivering friendly, authentic, caring, and thoughtful service (the FACT model). They refer to this as "Happy@Hampton™."

THE RITZ-CARLTON HOTEL COMPANY[9]

The Ritz-Carlton, one of the lodging brands of Marriott International, is the only hotel company to receive the Malcolm Baldrige National Quality Award and has done so twice.[10] Among the things the company did to win this coveted award—and continues to do—they

- provided 100 hours of customer service training for each employee annually;
- ensured check-in happens efficiently and quickly;
- developed a system called CARE (Clean And Repair Everything) to create the most defect-free guestrooms in the industry;
- ensured that a member of the service department broke away from his or her regular duties to help a guest with a maintenance request; and
- ensured every employee was the customer.

The Ritz-Carlton has three steps of service and 12 service values that employees are expected to learn and embrace, all which help ensure each moment of truth provides a positive customer experience. The three steps of service are:

1. Offer a warm and sincere greeting.

Antoine Chahwan, President of Hotel Operations for America's East Four Seasons Hotels & Resorts, one of the hotel companies most admired for its exceptional service, highlights the importance of selecting and motivating a passionate staff.

"The Four Seasons mantra, 'Treat others the way you want to be treated,' is the Golden Rule promulgated by the founder and Chairman, Isadore Sharp. Everybody wants to be understood. Everybody wants to be welcomed. Everybody wants to be pampered. And everybody wants to be respected. No matter where you go, people react to these principles the same way. So, we're looking for people to deliver magic. To do so people must have the right attitude, and that attitude must be in their heart. But you can't teach people to have a great attitude. We hire people because they have the right attitude, then we teach them the skills to deliver those experiences."

2. Address a guest by name (anticipate and fulfill each guest's needs).

3. Give a fond farewell (a sincere good-bye using the guest's name).

The 12 service values each employee is expected to embrace are:

1. Build strong relationships and create Ritz-Carlton guests for life.

2. Always be responsive to the expressed and unexpressed wishes and needs of guests.

3. Be empowered to create unique, memorable, and personal experiences for our guests.

4. Understand their role in achieving *Key Success Factors, Embracing Community Footprints*, and creating *The Ritz-Carlton Mystique*.

5. Continuously seek opportunities to innovate and improve The Ritz-Carlton experience.

6. Own and immediately resolve guest problems.

7. Create a work environment of teamwork and lateral service so that the needs of our guests and each other are met.

8. Recognize the opportunity to continuously learn and grow.

9. Be involved in the planning of the work that affects them.

10. Be proud of their professional appearance, language, and behavior.

11. Protect the privacy and security of guests, fellow employees, and the company's confidential information and assets.

12. Take responsibility for uncompromising levels of cleanliness and creating a safe and accident-free environment.

Ritz-Carlton is also credited with the introduction of the simple but highly impactful "10/5-foot rule" about consumer contact cited in chapter four. Again, this rule states "when 10 feet away make eye contact and within five feet, say hello."

Examples From Healthcare

Some healthcare service providers have developed and/or adopted similar efforts to deliver positive moments of truth in encounters with patients. These reveal how the adoption of select principles of hospitality can have a very positive impact on the patient experience.

CANCER TREATMENT CENTERS OF AMERICA GLOBAL, INC.™

Cancer Treatment Centers of America Global, Inc.® (CTCA), part of City of Hope, is a national network of hospitals and outpatient clinics that treats adult patients, typically with complex or advanced-stage cancer. Offering integrative cancer care, CTCA combines advanced surgery, radiation, chemotherapy, and immunotherapy with supportive therapies to enhance quality of life both during and after treatment. Its mission is to deliver patient-centric, compassionate care that yields superior clinical outcomes and high patient satisfaction.

From its inception, CTCA's primary objective has been to establish a distinctive brand of cancer care founded in the compassionate treatment of the entire patient, not just the patient's tumor. This corporate ethos is reflected in a singular service standard conceived by the chairman and embraced by all employees: the Mother Standard® of care. This is a promise to treat every patient with the same level of compassion one would demand for their mother if she ever required treatment. It is manifest in the way patients are served, from the moment they consider CTCA as a treatment provider, through the commencement, duration, and conclusion of treatment, and translates into memorable moments of truth.

- Every inquiry about diagnosis or treatment is handled live by a full-time patient empowerment representative. Whether by phone or online chat, at any hour of the day, seven days a week, these oncology information specialists provide a compassionate voice to actively engage anyone who contacts CTCA. Response times are monitored closely to ensure inquiries are handled with the same urgency expressed by callers. Calls are typically answered in less than three rings 24/7/365, holidays included. The specialists are highly trained and skilled at responding to questions, both general and CTCA-specific, about diagnoses, treatment options, care logistics, insurance, and related financial matters. And these brand ambassadors are trained to *not* screen out individuals who are either unable or unwilling to consider CTCA for treatment. Rather, even if someone does not fit CTCA's prospective patient profile, he or she is treated as someone who deserves their full attention with compassion and receives it.

- If permitted by the applicable insurance, once a patient has been scheduled for an appointment, the CTCA travel management team assists with travel arrangements. Patients who travel to one of the hospitals by plane or train are met by a uniformed CTCA representative at the destination terminal upon arrival, then transferred to the host hospital via private coach.

- Upon arrival at the hospital, patients are greeted by a lobby concierge whose sole job is to provide a warm, personal welcome—by name—and facilitate registration. Patients register at a writing desk where they receive a detailed schedule of their appointments and, if staying overnight, are personally escorted to their on-site hotel accommodations which have been designed to host caregivers and family as well.

- The servicescape of CTCA hospitals reflects the brand's resolute focus on the patient experience. From spacious, light-filled lobbies decorated to feel more like living rooms featuring soothing music from a grand piano to patient examination rooms designed to reduce anxiety, promote dialogue, and enhance comfort, the attention given to curating an environment conducive to whole-person well-being is evident.

- The compassionate way patients are treated at CTCA yields

memorable moments of truth as well. Staff are carefully selected and trained so they are committed to living the promise of the Mother Standard. Compelling examples occur every day: a nurse who volunteers to take a patient's anxious children out to a movie when it becomes apparent the children need a break from supporting their father's long day in the clinic; a physical therapist who pulls strings to get a star linebacker from the local NFL team to pay a surprise visit to a fan convalescing through surgical recovery; a care team that helps a bedridden patient stage the wedding she thought would never happen. Inspirational stories such as these are shared with colleagues during departmental "lineups" hosted in each department to recognize staff who have gone above and beyond in their delivery of the Mother Standard.

The impact of CTCA's commitment to engage patients in this unique manner is evident in several performance metrics:

- CTCA ranked third of 42 nationally recognized hospital systems rated in the YouGov BrandIndex survey of the most admired in the US behind only Mayo Clinic and Johns Hopkins Medicine, in 2020.[11]

- CTCA ranked in the 98th percentile of respondents who "would definitely recommend their hospital" and the 97th percentile of respondents who "gave their hospital a 9 or 10 on a 10-point scale" among the 2,790 hospitals surveyed in the national cohort of the July 2018 – June 2019 HCAHPS (Hospital Consumer Assessment of Hospitals and Healthcare Providers) survey.[12] (Note: HCAHPS scores are published every calendar quarter using data for the trailing four quarters of data.)

CLEVELAND CLINIC

Cleveland Clinic was the first major academic healthcare system to make the patient experience a strategic priority through the appointment of a Chief Experience Officer in 2007, and they were one of the first to establish an Office of Patient Experience, also in 2007. The Clinic strives to deliver great patient experiences—and moments of truth—by putting patients first.[13]

As defined on their website, the Patient First commitment involves four main aspects of engagement: safe care, high-value care, high-quality care, and patient satisfaction. Patient satisfaction derives from every aspect of a patient's engagement with the Clinic and includes not only their physical comfort, but educational, emotional, and spiritual needs as well. The Clinic addresses these by fielding teams of professionals working across multiple disciplines to ensure patient-centered care.

Shoemaker visited Cleveland Clinic and spent time with the different departments responsible for the patient experience. He noticed that every member of the staff was called a caregiver, not an employee. Everyone wore a caregiver badge, similar in size to the RN badges worn by most nurses. In addition, employee IDs were attached to a sleeve bearing the message, *Patient First*, in contrast to the ID sleeves used by many hospitals that feature just the hospital logo.

While this might not seem like a big difference, it is. The Patient First mantra reminds employees that patients are their main priority. The caregiver badge worn by all employees reinforces the conviction they are there to help patients regardless of their title or official role in the hospital. When patients see the Patient First message, they are reminded of the organization's commitment to their well-being.

Employee performance evaluations are also tied to service excellence including behaviors representative of the organization's culture as defined by its mission, vision, and values. Tying employee performance evaluations to service excellence helps ensure that all employees try to ensure both positive and memorable moments of truth.

UNIVERSITY OF TEXAS, MD ANDERSON CANCER CARE CENTER

The University of Texas MDACC also has a Chief Experience Officer, a position first staffed in 2017. MDACC continued their patient experience journey when, in 2012, Shoemaker—a professor in the University of Houston Hilton College of Hotel Administration at the time—was hired by the Division of Diagnostic Imaging to introduce hospitality principles into their division.

One of the outcomes resulting from Shoemaker's research was the development of the Anderson Care model, which introduced a protocol to make patients feel like a loved family member. A fundamental component of Anderson Care was the Anderson greeting acronym that guided all interactions between employees and patients. It was derived from the following behaviors:

A = Acknowledge
N = Nod
D = Delight
E = Eye Contact
R = Recognize
S = Smile
O = Orient
N = Nurture
C = Compassion
A = Assurance
R = Respect
E = Engage

All staff members were asked to display these behaviors to make each moment of truth both positive and memorable. In addition to the behaviors implied by the acronym, the Anderson Care model also prescribed the following:

- Respect patients' time.
- Respect patients' emotions.
- Respect patients' needs.
- Respect family and caregivers.
- Respect the disease.
- Respect each other.

The methodology introduced by MDACC to understand and improve the patient experience provides a useful guide for other healthcare service providers working to ensure positive and memorable moments of truth.

Hospitality "Moments of Truth" Principles in Healthcare

To illustrate a methodology healthcare service providers may use to ensure positive interaction between patients and employees, we provide a six-step overview of the application introduced by Shoemaker in his work with the University of Texas MDACC's Division of Diagnostic Imaging.[14]

STEP ONE: MEET WITH CARE UNIT MEMBERS

The first step was one of the most important: meet with members of every unit that was part of the continuum of care—from the staff who checked patients in, the nurses who administered the gadolinium-based contrast agent for the MRI and drew blood samples, to the technologists who took the images, the radiologists who read the images, and the staff who checked patients out. The goal of these initial meetings was to let everyone in the organization know why management was conducting the research and the related goals. It also provided an opportunity to discover how each group defined itself and others within the department.

This was important because the researchers did not want to alienate one group based on how they were defined by others. For example, in the first meeting, the radiologists defined the individuals who took the images as *technicians*. When the research team used this term to address this group, they immediately exclaimed, "Technicians fix toaster ovens. We are technologists; we take images of cancer!"

The barrier to collaboration on the project dissolved immediately once the radiologists started referring to this group as *technologists*.

STEP TWO: CREATE JOURNEY MAPS

The next step involved creating a series of journey maps to identify moments of truth. (Journey mapping was discussed in chapter three.) All departments in diagnostic imaging were involved in this step, as each had different moments of truth. In order to ensure that patients also provided input on this important step, in depth interviews and focus groups were conducted with patients. They were asked to list every step of their experience from the time they made their appointment to the time they got home.

STEP THREE: SET SERVICE STANDARDS FOR EACH MOMENT OF TRUTH

Once journey maps were developed, the service standards for each moment of truth were set. These were determined by asking each unit of the diagnostic imaging division the following questions:

- What is the end-result or consequence of the interaction from the service provider's and patients' perspectives?
- What actions undertaken by each unit provide a great experience during this moment of truth?
- What actions undertaken by guests' match those undertaken by the service provider? For example, consider the check-in process as a guest action; what then is the corresponding action from the service provider? Where necessary, add corresponding actions by the service provider to ensure guests' needs are met. For example, a guest action may be, "I get a warm blanket from one of the staff." If the action, "delivering a warm blanket to a guest," is not listed on the service provider side, it should be added.

STEP FOUR: INCORPORATE THE RATER SYSTEM

What we referred to previously as *planning your work* came next. It involved deconstructing each identified interaction between patients and employees and then incorporating one or more of the components of the RATER system (Reliability, Assurance, Tangible, Empathy, and Responsiveness) to remind patients they were receiving superior service.

This step must be designed by the employees who will deliver the service to help ensure they embrace the process and deliver on the service standards, even when management is not present. For example, at MDACC, the team taking care of patients prior to their MRI scanning realized no one person was responsible for checking on them while they waited for their images to be taken. The team then decided to have each team member take turns looking after patients while they waited. To keep track of who was responsible at any given time, the team decided to use a 30-minute sand timer they passed like a torch from member to member. One day a member dropped the sand timer, and it broke. Another member rushed to buy a new one during his break.

Had management said to the team, "You will use a sand timer to keep track of whose turn it is to interact with the patients," instead of letting the team take the initiative, it is doubtful the broken sand timer would have been replaced, certainly not as quickly.

STEP FIVE: TRAIN STAFF TO DELIVER

Staff were trained to deliver the superior service that had been designed. This is what we referred to in chapter one as "working your plan." Recall the Ritz Carlton provides over 100 hours of training per employee per year. According to Finley Cotrone, PhD, an Associate Professor in Residence at UNLV, and former executive at Four Seasons and MGM Resorts International, there are several key factors to a successful training program:

- The organization must have clear service delivery standards that outline the minimum level of service required in each role. These standards are separate from the technical aspects of the job.
- Staff must be given opportunities to practice the service standards before putting them into action with patients and caregivers.

- Emotional connection and empathy must be present in the standards as well as taught and practiced "off stage."
- A connection must be made between the service standards and the mission, vision, and values of the organization.
- The culture must reinforce the service standards as "the way we do things here."
- Coaching and positive reinforcement in real-time should be provided as much as possible.
- Service failures should be used as training and coaching opportunities to teach staff how to make better choices.

STEP SIX: DESIGN INSTRUMENTS OF ASSESSMENT

Finally, step six prepared to assess the success or failure of hospitality "moments of truth" principles by designing the appropriate instruments, such as surveys. We discuss other recommended methods in chapter six.

Importance of Understanding

As stated in chapter two, respondents in our Gap Survey confirmed an intuitive assumption: knowing the cost of the service before it is purchased is an important part of the engagement both hospitality and healthcare service providers have with customers. We also underscored how the opacity of pricing for healthcare services renders this understanding problematic. But the understanding sought by consumers extends well beyond the cost of the service to include many other important aspects of engagement. They wonder, *Will the service align with my expectations? Will it satisfy my needs? Who will perform the service? What are their credentials? Should I consider alternative providers? What happens if things don't go as planned?*

These considerations coalesce to yield a discomforting anxiety and corresponding need for information that will allay the related concerns. The importance of dialogue to obtain this information is evident in how our Gap Survey respondents rated the overall importance of, "The opportunity to ask questions about things I don't understand," as 8.3 on a 10-point scale. This was exceeded by only two other considerations: "The invoice I receive is consistent with my expectation," (8.47 on a 10-point scale) and "Quick resolution of any problems I express about my experience," (8.40 on a 10-point scale).

Clearly, consumers of hospitality services are much more able to access and interpret information about the services they plan to consume than consumers of healthcare services. This is due, in part, to their familiarity with those services, borne of previous experience staying in hotels, dining out, and so on. Inquiries about how specific accommodations differ are easy to address both verbally and visually. Questions about unfamiliar items on a dinner menu are easily answered by well-trained wait staff. And if someone is not familiar with a desired service, there is typically a plethora of easily understood information available online about the nature and quality of the service, often accompanied by colorful commentary from others who have already consumed it.

This is less true in healthcare. Patients generally have little or no familiarity with the vocabulary of either diagnoses or treatments. Online searches to enhance understanding may be modestly helpful, but difficult to understand. This lack of understanding explains the high rating ascribed to the importance of the following statement by respondents in our Gap Survey: "The provider explains things without making me feel rushed," (8.1 on a 10-point scale). Respondents were significantly more likely to agree that this statement applied more to visiting a physician's office than their experience with any of the other four service categories rated: hotel/motel/resort, dining out, visiting a hospital, and visiting a walk-in clinic. (Note: A complete set of figures from our Gap Survey may be found at www.hospitablehealthcare.com.)

The previous data underscore an inherent conflict between the way consumers of healthcare services want to be served and the way healthcare service providers are managed, or incentivized, to serve them. Patients place a high value on the time spent with clinicians to explain their diagnosis and treatment. Yet, most healthcare providers are inclined—even encouraged—to serve patients as quickly as possible. Their performance evaluations by senior management may include a critical review of the average amount of time spent with patients with demerits given if or when this exceeds the targeted key performance indicator (KPI). Yet, there is considerable evidence in the published literature that confirms time spent by clinicians with patients has a positive effect on patient satisfaction. In fact, Yesawich conducted several studies for a national provider of oncology care that revealed the amount of time clinicians spent with patients explaining such aspects as their diagnosis, treatment, and potential side-effects was the single most important contributor to overall patient satisfaction.

The conundrum of time spent with patients versus service velocity faces practically every healthcare service provider, however. They must therefore weigh the short-term benefits of achieving greater patient velocity, and presumably revenue, against the longer-term benefits of achieving higher patient satisfaction and provider/facility loyalty. For example, we understand some radiologists now receive scorecards tracking their moments of inactivity. The results are compared to those of their colleagues to determine their relative efficiency and subsequently considered in performance reviews.

As we reveal when discussing the power of customer loyalty in chapter seven, we believe that investing the time to answer patients' questions about clinical issues they don't understand—in an unhurried manner—will enhance patient satisfaction in the short-term, and loyalty in the long term.

At Your Service

But what about time spent answering non-clinical questions posed by patients? Again, we look to the hospitality industry for clues.

The most successful hospitality service providers address guests' desire to ask questions about things they don't understand by offering convenient access to an employee who is trained specifically to serve in this role: a concierge. The concierge is a font of knowledge about everything from property policies and procedures to area attractions, dining options, business services, and transportation. He or she is typically stationed in a highly visible location of the host facility to invite inquiries or readily accessible online or by phone. The sole mission of a concierge is to enhance guest satisfaction by facilitating guests' access to information that may not be readily available or understood.

Several hospital systems now offer concierge-like services to patients such as assistance with transportation, dining, housing, or other services that may be sought by patients when receiving treatment. This is not to be confused with *concierge medicine* which is a private form of practice wherein physicians charge patients an additional fee, typically offered on a subscription basis, for privileged access to their services.

Adoption of this beneficial service doesn't necessarily require additional staffing or payroll if patient volumes are insufficient to support a dedicated full-time equivalent employee. Rather, the role may be assigned to an existing member of the administrative staff who possesses the knowledge and people skills to engage with patients successfully. Alternatively, providers may offer access to virtual concierge services on days or times that don't conflict with other important obligations. Although in-person engagement is always preferable, the actual form of engagement is less important than simply making information available to patients who are seeking clarification or guidance.

Understanding Cost

Earlier we revealed that, "Understanding the invoice I receive," and "The invoice I receive is consistent with my expectation," were rated most important among the entire battery of 24 sentiments measured in our Gap Survey. We also posited reasons for the transparency of hospitality service pricing and opacity of healthcare service pricing, especially in the hospital setting. The US government's fledging effort to force hospitals to reveal prices for many services notwithstanding, we believe healthcare service pricing will become more transparent as a result of the groundswell of consumer advocacy on this issue, increased competition among providers, and the growing influence of social media. Insurance companies who actually pay the service providers—commonly known as payors—are now under pressure by the US Centers for Medicare and Medicaid Services (CMS) to publish the costs of many healthcare services they have negotiated with providers resulting from the Transparency of Coverage rule that took effect July 1, 2022. So, how may healthcare service providers address the inevitability of this outcome in a manner that enhances patient satisfaction? Again, we look to the hospitality industry for guidance.

Unlike booking a medical procedure, guests of hotels, resorts, and transportation companies know the price of services at the time of booking, typically inclusive of taxes and incidental fees. Furthermore, the quoted price is guaranteed unless the roster of desired services is amended. A similar process could be adopted by healthcare service providers based on the schedule of services planned. Even if a patient requires additional tests or other procedures that may not be known at the time of booking, a pro forma estimate of the charges could be provided. One that reveals the payment the provider expects to receive from the payor—government or applicable insurance company—versus the expected obligation of the patient would be especially helpful. Patients could be notified that any required adjustments would be made on the final bill. Such an arrangement would diminish the unpleasant surprise that accompanies receipt of a bill for healthcare services for which no estimate of the cost was provided in advance.

The prevalence of this problem was revealed in a 2020 survey conducted by Waystar.[15] An alarming 56% of respondents stated they had received a "surprise" medical bill. Most hotels and resorts provide these pro forma estimates at the time of booking, and once again prior to check-out on the guest's in-room television and/or a branded mobile app. Healthcare service providers could and should do the same.

Consumers' desire for clarification of pricing and/or other aspects of services they may not understand is, not surprisingly, more pronounced in healthcare than hospitality as revealed in Figure 5.3. This is a logical reflection of their concern about both the unknown cost of the services and potential consequences of things going wrong with treatment.

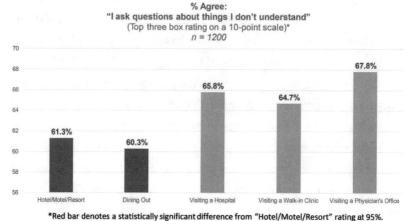

*Red bar denotes a statistically significant difference from "Hotel/Motel/Resort" rating at 95%.

Figure 5.3: Asking questions to enhance understanding.

Privacy is Not a Privilege

It will come as no surprise to readers that the rating of, "The people I interact with respect my privacy," equals that of, "The ability to ask questions about things I don't understand," (8.3 on a 10-point scale). It is equally interesting to note that respondents in our Gap Survey cited the staff in physicians' offices as most respectful of this concern.

The importance of protecting the privacy of patients' health-related information was memorialized with the passage of HIPAA, enacted by the US Congress in 1996. The law stipulated how personally identifiable information maintained by healthcare providers and healthcare insurance companies must be protected from both fraud and theft. It prohibits healthcare providers and healthcare businesses from disclosing this protected information to anyone other than the patient and the patient's authorized representatives without the patient's consent.

Concerns about the way all service providers capture, share, and protect user information have also amplified in recent years, given the frequent reports of data breaches in practically every industry. In the European Union, this concern was the catalyst for the introduction of the most rigorous law enacted to enhance personal data privacy to date: the General Data Protection Regulation, which became effective in May of 2018. In the US, the California Consumer Privacy Act of 2018 was enacted to provide residents of California with similar privacy protection.

Given the important issues related to data privacy—not just protected health information— all service providers should now solicit, curate, and manage personal data only with the prior consent of guests, whether required by law or otherwise. Observance of this principle will not only ensure compliance if such action is legislated, but also enable providers to facilitate future transactions and, importantly, personalize the delivery of service that aligns with guests' preferences. As stated earlier, the most successful hospitality service providers have refined techniques to facilitate transactions and enhance guest recognition while respecting the privacy of guests. We believe healthcare service providers could achieve similar results while remaining compliant with HIPAA by addressing many of the administrative aspects of service delivery, as discussed previously.

Personal Worth

The most admired hospitality service providers focus relentlessly on ensuring that they meet, and hopefully exceed, the expectations of guests. They also work tirelessly to make guests feel good about themselves, another less obvious outcome. Now, this may sound like an unusual service goal yet, if achieved, represents one of the most important residuals of positive customer engagement because it enhances customer loyalty.

"We're glad you're here" has become a hackneyed expression embraced by many hospitality service providers, but the underlying sentiment is especially powerful when guests conclude it is genuine, based on the attitudes and behaviors of those who deliver the service. That is why many lodging and restaurant operators train their frontline staff to express sincere thanks for each guest's patronage, especially as their engagement is about to conclude at checkout or just prior to departure.

Respondents in our Gap Survey confirmed the importance of sensing this sentiment, rating, "The provider appreciates my business," at a 7.95 on a 10-point scale. Genuine expressions of thanks delivered coincidental with presentation of an invoice are commonplace in hotels and restaurants. Similar expressions of thanks in healthcare appear less frequent or, if delivered at all, less genuine. At times they come across as if the patient should be grateful for receiving treatment. A more genuine expression of thanks, delivered in a consistent manner, would go a long way toward concluding engagements with healthcare service providers in a positive, memorable manner.

As was discussed in chapter four, the Ritz-Carlton is particularly adept at making guests feel good about themselves by doing such things as training staff to make eye contact, acknowledging their presence with a gracious greeting, preferably by name and, when appropriate, offering a compliment on their preferences or appearance. Respondents to our Gap Survey help us understand the importance of this sentiment, rating, "The provider makes me feel good about myself," 7.3 on a 10-point scale. It is interesting to note that physicians' offices do this far better than all other service providers measured in the survey.

How to Engage Patients to Deliver Hospitable Healthcare

The importance of customer engagement has been acknowledged

since the reign of King Louis XIV of France who is famously credited with saying, "Everything starts with the customer." In more recent times, Steve Jobs said, "Get closer than ever to your customers. So close that you tell them what they need well before they realize it themselves."[16]

In previous chapters, we discussed the RATER system as a tool to remind customers they are receiving quality service. To use the RATER system effectively, however, the service provider must actively engage with customers. Below are some of the most important actions healthcare service providers should implement to create a culture of positive engagement with their patients:

- Teach your team members the 14 key words of a service encounter developed by Edward Mady from The Beverly Hills Hotel: *remember me, recognize me, anticipate my needs, give me what I want on time.*

- Introduce an acronym that reflects your commitment to enhancing patient satisfaction that is easy for your staff to remember and recite—recall our discussion of Anderson Care. Things easily remembered are more likely to be acted upon than those that aren't.

- Develop and introduce service standards that specify the minimum level of service expected in each staff role. These standards should be developed in collaboration with the employees, who ultimately deliver the service standards, and with the patients, who will be the beneficiaries of those service standards.

- Ensure a connection between the service standards and your mission, vision, and values. The behaviors that are repeated over and over create and define the culture of your organization. Patients and staff members will clearly recognize if there is a disconnect between what you say and what you do.

- Present patients with a final bill that clearly explains the reason for any variance from the estimate they received prior to arrival. Remember, engagement happens throughout the customer lifecycle, and they usually remember the last interaction most vividly. This is typically the presentation of the bill. That is why upscale restaurants serve excellent coffee, tea, and a complimentary sweet at the conclusion of meal service. These are the last tastes most guests remember.

- Minimize the use of incomprehensible medical jargon and communicate in layman's terms so patients feel comfortable asking questions about things they don't understand. True engagement occurs when the two parties communicate with the same vocabulary.

- Introduce a satisfaction guarantee for services where the outcome is generally predictable and controllable. Such a guarantee would communicate the provider's confidence in the quality of the service experience delivered and build patients' trust in the expertise of the provider. Positive engagement cannot happen without trust.

CHAPTER 6

Evaluate: The Second *E* in PAEER

"We all need people who will give us feedback. That's how we improve."

– BILL GATES

What Do the Data Mean?

HAVING PREPARED FOR GUESTS' ARRIVAL, anticipated their expectations and anxieties, and implemented proven techniques to enhance their satisfaction once engaged, we are now ready to address the critical question of performance. *How well did we do? How do we know? Were guests satisfied with the service they received? How will they share this information with others? Can we do even better?*

This chapter answers these important questions with the second *E* in our PAEER model: *Evaluate.*

Patient Feedback in Healthcare

One corollary of the "information everywhere" environment in which we now live is customers' desire to review quality ratings of the healthcare service providers they consider for treatment. Their online search behavior affirms this.

According to a 2019 survey conducted by PatientPop, 70% of patients consider online reviews crucial when selecting a healthcare provider.[1] Similar results were revealed in the 2020 Master Patient

Experience Survey conducted by Software Advice:[2]

- 90% of patients use online reviews to evaluate physicians.
- Almost three quarters (71%) use online reviews as the first step in finding a new doctor.
- Consistent with our theory that patients are reticent to criticize medical professionals, only 1% of patients leave "very negative" reviews on healthcare provider websites, and just 10% leave "somewhat negative" reviews.

And in 2021, a survey conducted by REPUGEN yielded similar results: 81% of patients considered online reviews when selecting a healthcare provider.[3] Our Gap Survey confirmed what most practitioners believe intuitively as well: comments about healthcare service providers posted on social media are reviewed by a significant percentage of consumers, although fewer than those who review comments posted about hospitality service providers, as revealed in Figure 6.1.

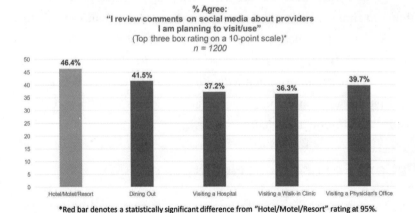

% Agree:
"I review comments on social media about providers
I am planning to visit/use"
(Top three box rating on a 10-point scale)*
n = 1200

*Red bar denotes a statistically significant difference from "Hotel/Motel/Resort" rating at 95%.

Figure 6.1: Review of comments on social media about service providers.

Given the importance of ratings and opinions documented by customers, we find it curious that less than half of the adults we surveyed reported requests for feedback on their experiences with hospitals and walk-in clinics. That is significantly lower than the percentage who receive such requests from hotels and resorts. Physicians' offices appear more likely than other healthcare service providers to solicit feedback, presumably because of the more trusting relationship patients form with personal care physicians over time. Again, fewer than 50% of consumers acknowledge receiving requests from these providers, as revealed in Figure 6.2.

Restaurants are least likely to request feedback from patrons. This reflects the transient nature of their clientele, although restaurant reservation services such as OpenTable and The Fork now request feedback from all guests who use these booking services as a matter of routine.

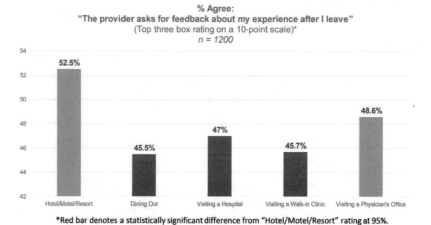

Figure 6.2: Requests for customer feedback by service providers.

Why more healthcare service providers don't routinely solicit feedback from their patients is a mystery. Possible reasons include the staff time required to manage data collection, the lack of expertise in survey design and data analysis to discern actionable insights, the expense of activating and maintaining such programs, or perhaps the hubris displayed by some providers who believe they don't need to ask patients about their experiences because they are the only qualified arbiters of excellent patient care. Years ago, hospitality service providers expressed similar concerns, yet discovering the value of guest feedback when charting a course toward higher guest satisfaction silenced those objections.

The HCAHPS Conundrum

Most hospitals have access to a common source of patient feed-back: the Hospital Consumer Assessment of Healthcare Providers and Systems (HCAHPS) survey of in-patient care implemented by US CMS beginning in October 2006 with initial data reported in March 2008.[4] This standardized and publicly reported survey of the types of encounters patients have with their hospital providers is national in scope and yields normative performance data for comparative purposes. According to CMS, the primary objective of the survey is "to produce data about patients' perspectives of care that allow objective and meaningful comparisons of hospitals on topics that are important to consumers." Conducted monthly with samples of patients drawn from each participating hospital, the results are reported quarterly and serve as one of the metrics evaluated by CMS to calculate incentive payments for hospitals in the Hospital Value-Based Purchasing program, as stipulated in the Patient Protection and Affordable Care Act of 2010.

The core HCAHPS survey instrument consists of 29 questions crafted to evaluate how patients experienced the delivery of care, not how satisfied they were with their care. This is an important distinction. Most questions probe how patients engaged with their clinical teams of physicians and nurses, the responsiveness of those teams to patient requests, pain management and medications. They did not inquire about such factors as facility design, amenities, ease of parking, the selection or quality of cuisine, concierge services, or many of the other variables known to affect patient satisfaction. Questions about important features such as the accessibility of appointments, clinic wait times, environmental design considerations, price transparency, comprehensible invoices for services rendered, and prompt resolution of billing disputes are conspicuously absent.

The difference between experience and satisfaction is frequently cited as a deficiency of the HCAHPS survey. It is one of the primary reasons many participating hospitals supplement the mandatory questions with additional questions intended to discern the level of satisfaction felt by patients. Healthcare service providers should applaud CMS's efforts to continually refine the relevance of HCAHPS metrics, however, as there is no national equivalent of comparable methodological rigor available in the hospitality industry.

Several healthcare service providers are now experimenting with data collection at different points of intervention during a patient's typical visit or course of care to deconstruct the gestalt of patient satisfaction into discrete, actionable events. Their underlying assumption is that each event presents an opportunity to improve patient satisfaction. Concerns about the accuracy of feedback solicited several days after the delivery of care have also elevated interest in experimentation with this type of data collection.

One very interesting finding from our Gap Study appears in Figure 6.3. The data reveal consumers believe hospitality service providers also make it easier to resolve disputes when problems occur. This clearly contrasts with their belief about dispute resolution by healthcare service providers.

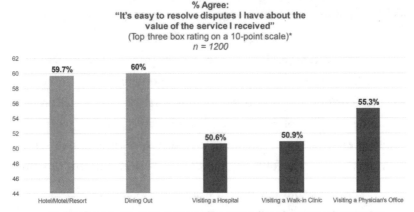

*Red bar denotes a statistically significant difference from "Hotel/Motel/Resort" rating at 95%.

Figure 6.3: Ease of dispute resolution with service providers.

One reason for the differences between hospitality and healthcare service providers on these important service variables is that hospitality service providers are generally very eager for customers to provide feedback. Another is they have implemented sophisticated monitoring systems that examine potential gaps between service expectations and delivery on a regular basis to guide continuous improvement. Recurring gaps are identified, addressed, and closed quickly. Examples of the systems and procedures notable hospitality service providers use to achieve these results are discussed next.

Problem Detection and Resolution in Hospitality

Hospitality service providers have invested considerable time, effort, and money in the techniques they employ to solicit feedback that may be used to enhance guest satisfaction. These include aggregate ratings of the overall guest experience, as well as component ratings of discrete moments of truth. Most solicit the participation of all guests—not just a sample of guests—and the resulting data are evaluated with reference to predetermined key performance indicators (KPIs). These KPIs are then compared to other properties providing service of comparable quality and/or competing for the same clientele. Hospitality industry executives call these other properties the *competitive set*.

For example, several hospitality service providers with whom the authors have worked believe that before an organization can measure whether customers are satisfied, it must first possess a comprehensive understanding of who those customers are, as well as their travel habits, preferences, and intentions. We therefore recommend service providers first ask the following questions to discern this information:

- What does your client need from your organization?
- What does your client want from your organization?
- What does your client expect from your organization?
- We recommend supplementing the information gathered with the following questions:

- Which clients do business with us, directly or indirectly?
- Which services do they purchase or use, and what actions must they take to do so?
- If clients didn't visit our organization, with what other organizations would they visit?
- What is the overall value of our offer to the client?
- What are the key drivers of client satisfaction?
- Which product or service attributes have the greatest potential to increase client satisfaction?
- Which performance changes will increase client satisfaction versus just being seen as improvements that are simply nice to have?

Understanding customers and then tailoring service offerings to deliver on the features that customers consider most important involves the following three principles:

1. Systematically benchmark and track guest satisfaction through a carefully designed survey sent to each guest shortly after staying at or dining with a specific property.

2. Share and review survey outcomes broadly within the organization and hold team members accountable for resolving any issues quickly.

3. Continuously adapt and improve services to meet evolving customer needs.

Hilton Worldwide tracks customer satisfaction over repeated administration of its post-departure survey with a proprietary metric: a satisfaction and loyalty tracking (SALT) score. Based upon conversations with current and former Hilton employees, plus having received surveys from Hilton after staying at a Hilton property, it can be stated that these scores derive from a variety of metrics related to different aspects of each guest's stay. Questions include the following, which are just a view of the many items measured:

- Overall, how satisfied were you with your stay? Please use any number on a one "not at all satisfied" to a 10 "very satisfied" scale.

- Overall, how likely are you to return to this hotel if your travels bring you back to this area? Please use any number on a one "not at all likely to return to this hotel" to 10 "extremely likely to return to this hotel" scale.

- Overall, how likely are you recommend Hilton to someone else if they were to need similar services? Please use a one for "a place I definitely won't recommend" up to a 10 "a place I definitely will recommend" scale.

- Overall, how satisfied were you with each of the following during your stay? Please use any number on a one "not at all satisfied" to a 10 "very satisfied" scale:

  The quality of the service you received.

  The attentiveness and helpfulness of the staff who assisted you.

  The cleanliness of your room.

  The friendliness of the staff.

  The length of time it took for you to check-in.

Many hospitality service providers engage Medallia, an enterprise software company that focuses on tapping into customer signals. Those signals are turned into prescriptive actions that improve the customer experience, enabling them to measure overall customer satisfaction with their experience.

Medallia uses sophisticated technology to capture multiple experience signals across the entire customer journey, not just data from periodic surveys. These signals are gleaned from different systems such as POS data, CRM data, and call center interactions; channels such as social media posts on Twitter, Facebook, and Instagram; in-house technology; third-party sources; as well as direct and indirect feedback such as found with Hilton's SALT scores. Data scraped from the worldwide web is referred to as *unstructured*, while data collected through traditional survey methods is referred to as *structured*. This information is then evaluated to gain a 360-degree view of guest sentiment.

Medallia details where and how signal data should be captured in the eBook, *Early Warning Signals: How Experience Signals Can Drive Your Business Forward*.[5] The components are illustrated in Figure 6.4.

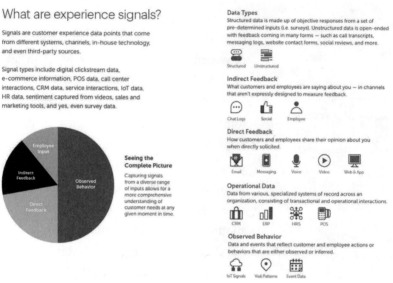

Figure 6.4: Customer experience signals tracked by Medallia. Used with permission from Medallia, Inc.

Another firm many hospitality service providers engage to measure guest satisfaction is Qualtrics. Like Medallia, Qualtrics has developed a suite of software products that enables providers to monitor real time tracking across essentially every part of the customer journey.[6] These tools provide information on where customers may be unhappy along the journey.

A key credential of both organizations—and really all companies that offer experience management software—is the ability to capture comments across all relevant channels, then automatically sort the

Toni Land, MBA, BSN, and CPXP, is Head of Clinical Healthcare Experience at Medallia, Inc. She has more than 30 years of experience in numerous healthcare settings including nursing, home care, medical practice, performance improvement, management, and as Chief Patient Experience & Quality Officer for a major healthcare system.

"Trust is foundational to the patient experience and engagement. As organizations build trust, they see an increase in patients' adherence to their plan of care and improved patient outcomes.

The key drivers of improving experiences and building trust we've identified through our data and work with leading healthcare brands around the world include communication and respect, listening, and taking action.

Communication and Respect: Patients and families are looking for honest, proactive, communication in words they can understand and in their preferred mode of communication.

Listening: This is a two-pronged requirement. Most clinicians interrupt a patient within 30 seconds after asking the purpose of their visit."

comments by: (1) sentiment—positive, neutral, or negative; and (2) common theme—comments about check-in, price value relations, and so on.

There is yet another tool hospitality service providers use to measure guest satisfaction, one that is both simple and inexpensive. Hospitality service providers have called this the *problem impact tree*—although the authors of this text are not sure about the provenance of this term. The problem impact tree is illustrated in Figure 6.5

Adding one just item to existing customer surveys will make it easy to determine how many guests didn't experience a problem, and among those who did, how many of them reported it to staff. It also reveals how well the service provider responded to those problems.

As reflected in Figure 6.5, this item asks customers to "Please indicate if you reported any problems during your visit and, if so, how they were resolved." Their responses yield the following information:

- the percentage of guests who had a problem during their stay;

- of those who had a problem, the percentage who reported the problem to management;

- of those who reported a problem, the percentage who claimed the problem was solved to their satisfaction; and

- of those who reported a problem, the percentage who claimed the problem was not solved to their satisfaction.

Hospitality service providers use the results of this question to determine the impact of service failures on other measures usually collected in post-departure surveys. For example, Figure 6.6 illustrates the impact service failures have on three critical customer sentiments: (1) guests' overall satisfaction with the experience; (2) guests' willingness to visit frequently; and (3) whether guests would "definitely recommend" the property to friends. As implied by the results, management should

Toni Land CONT.

"So, during patient encounters clinicians need to take the time to listen, without interrupting. They should also ask both patients and caregivers for feedback on their experience, listen to that feedback, then use it to create action plans for improvement.

Action: Patients and caregivers want to know they have been heard and that their clinical team is acting on their feedback. Consistent follow up about both good and bad experiences builds trust and continues the feedback cycle for on-going improvement."

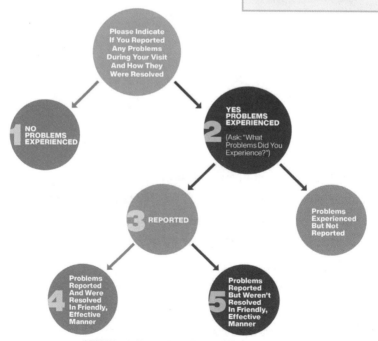

© 2022 Hospitable Healthcare Partners, LLC.

Figure 6.5: Service problem detection and resolution.

encourage customers to inform staff when service failures occur and have a plan in place to rectify any failures promptly and satisfactorily.

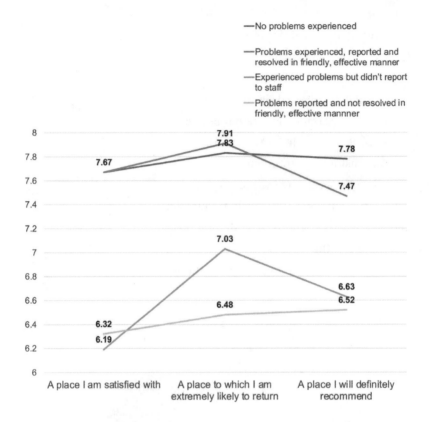

Figure 6.6: Customer responses to service problem detection and resolution.

Another metric popular with hospitality service providers is the customer satisfaction index (CSI). This index allows providers to: (1) determine how well the organization performs on features important to customers; and (2) measure how the organization is perceived relative to its competition.

To illustrate this method, consider a case study undertaken by Shoemaker focusing on hotel casinos in Atlantic City, New Jersey. To determine the relative importance of the features to be measured, guests were asked three questions at the time of check-in:

1. What was important in your decision to choose this hotel casino over another?

2. If you weren't staying here, where would you have stayed?

3. What was the reason for your visit? (This question was asked because the sponsor of the study wanted to look only at gamblers. Data collected from those who were visiting for other reasons were excluded.)

The analysis revealed ten features to be most important for gamblers visiting Atlantic City. It also revealed five other hotel casinos where customers would have stayed if they had not stayed in the one where they received the survey. Armed with these insights, management developed a survey instrument that was distributed to a random sample of previous guests whose contact information was recorded in the hotel's database.

The CSI derives from a weighted average of the important features and performance scores on the various property attributes. As a result, hotel management obtained valuable knowledge about which features were most important to guests and how guests perceived the property's performance on those features. Management also benefited from results that revealed how guests perceived their competitors' performance on the same attributes. Additional detail on the calculation of the CSI may be found in Appendix C.

The CSI analysis also enables management to discover attributes that are not important, even if managers think they are. By plotting importance versus performance, hospitality service providers discover features in which they are overinvesting or underinvesting. This is illustrated in Figure 6.7 using data from another proprietary casino study. The applicable data were used to construct an "importance versus performance" map for one of the properties.

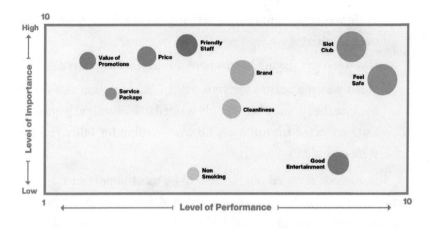

© 2022 Hospitable Healthcare Partners, LLC.

Figure 6.7: Actionable insights using a customer satisfaction index.

The *x*-axis in Figure 6.7 is the performance axis, and the *y*-axis is the importance axis. The variables appearing in red in the upper left-hand corner are important to customers, but the service provider performs poorly on them, indicating management should initiate improvement strategies. Management should monitor any changes in the ratings of the variables appearing in green in the upper-right quadrant, as these are important to customers and the organization is perceived to perform well on them.

Management doesn't need to address the green item in the lower left quadrant (non-smoking), as it is not important to customers and the organization's performance on this variable is not perceived to be negative.

The item appearing in the lower right quadrant (good entertainment) is red because it is not important to customers, even though the organization performs well on it. Available resources should therefore be spent to improve the variables appearing in red in the upper left quadrant, given their known importance to guests.

These examples illustrate ways in which hospitality service providers make it easy for customers to provide feedback, both positive and negative. As illustrated, not only do hospitality firms make it easy for customers to give feedback, but they also attempt to fix any service failures quickly. If customers know the service provider wants to hear any complaints and is willing to fix them, they will be more inclined to express their dissatisfaction when things go awry. This was the inspiration for the 100% service guarantee adopted by Hampton Inn, as discussed in chapter two.

We believe similar analyses may be undertaken in any market area where there are multiple healthcare facilities serving multiple patients. The methodology and procedures would be the same, but the questions and brands would obviously be different.

Spreading The Word

Word of mouth, of course, has always existed as a force in commerce. The advent and rapid adoption of social media—one of the ways "information everywhere" has enabled word of mouth to become more powerful— has encouraged service providers to rely less on traditional advertising and place more emphasis on soliciting new customers through the placement and promotion of word-of-mouth commentary. This form of advertising occurs when a provider's customers talk or post about the brand in favorable ways to their friends or others on social media channels. Research presented in the *Nielsen Global Trust in Advertising Report* (2015)[7] illustrates the importance of this type of communication:

- 83% of online respondents in 60 countries reported they trust the recommendations of friends and family.

- 66% of the respondents stated they trust consumer opinions posted online.

Word of mouth is a critical measure for all service providers because of the intangible nature of services. Recall the characteristics of services discussed in chapter one: intangibility, heterogeneity, and simultaneous production and consumption. These characteristics make it impossible for consumers to evaluate the service prior to purchase. Because of this, consumers seek advice and opinions from others, as described above. Think about the last time you chose a hotel, a restaurant, or a doctor. How did you decide? Opinions you solicited from friends, family and associates probably influenced your decision. The results of our Gap Study confirm this thesis as well.

The proliferation of social media has amplified the time-honored tradition of either praising or disparaging the service providers we use. But unlike just a few short years ago when one's sphere of influence was basically restricted to family, friends, and business associates, social media have provided engaged consumers with access to a digital megaphone that has practically unlimited reach. The data in Figure 6.8 reveal most adults actively share accounts of their encounters with the five types of service providers measured in our Gap Survey, although significantly less so about their experiences with hospitals and walk-in clinics. Again, we posit the reason for the latter is consumers' lack of context for evaluating these experiences with confidence versus their more frequent exposure to, hence familiarity with hotels and restaurants.

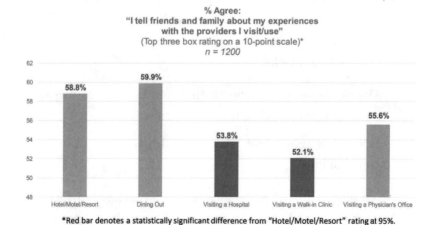

% Agree:
"I tell friends and family about my experiences
with the providers I visit/use"
(Top three box rating on a 10-point scale)*
n = 1200

*Red bar denotes a statistically significant difference from "Hotel/Motel/Resort" rating at 95%.

Figure 6.8: Sharing information about experiences with service providers.

Word of mouth is supercharged via social media when someone is sufficiently pleased or aggrieved with the service they received from either hospitality or healthcare service providers. This is especially true for experiences with hotels, resorts, and restaurants and, once again, less so for hospitals and walk-in clinics, as revealed in Figure 6.9.

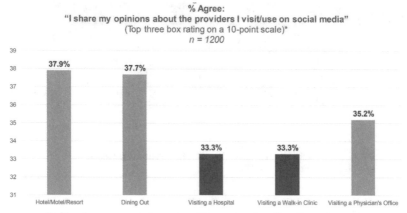

Figure 6.9: Use of social media to share information about experiences with service providers.

Given the importance of word of mouth to both new customer acquisition and brand reputation, however, it is important to understand how to measure it.

Measuring Word of Mouth

The *Net Promoter Score* (NPS) is a quantitative proxy for *word of mouth* that measures customers' willingness to recommend a service provider. Fedrick Reichheld of Bain and Company invented this measure in 2013.[8] Instead of using a 1 to 10 scale as discussed above, however, the NPS score derives from a 0 to 10 scale where 0 is "not at all likely to recommend" and 10 is "very likely to recommend." The NPS is calculated using following formula: $(p \geq 9) - (p \leq 6) = $ NPS, or the percentage of respondents rating the provider a nine or 10 (most positive) minus the percentage of respondents rating the provider a six or less (most negative). This is illustrated in Figure 6.10. Some healthcare providers such as Mayo Clinic supplement the NPS with additional insight to yield greater precision when assessing patient sentiment, however.

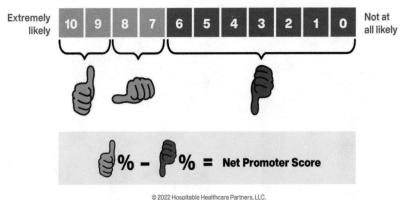

© 2022 Hospitable Healthcare Partners, LLC.

Figure 6.10: Calculating a Net Promoter Score.

Calculating the Value of Word of Mouth

To calculate the value of word of mouth, whether using NPS or some other technique, one needs the following information according to Roger Hallowell and Abby Hansen of Harvard Business School:[9]

- the likelihood that the customer will refer the provider;
- the number of people to whom the recommendation will be made;
- the percentage of referrals who are empathetic (those who may act on what they hear);
- the probability that those who are empathetic will buy the service; and
- the lifetime value of the customer.

As an example, Shoemaker calculated the value of word of mouth in a proprietary study for a hotel casino from responses to the following questions:

- How many people will you tell about your visit to this hotel casino?
- Of the people you will tell, how many can act upon this recommendation?
- What percentage of those who can act will stay and gamble at this hotel casino?

Results revealed that on average, participants would tell 8.3 people; they believed 5.1 people had the ability to act upon this recommendation; and 64% of those would stay and gamble. Management previously estimated the lifetime value of the average gaming customer at the hotel casino was $11,271. The results of this study revealed that word of mouth referrals made by satisfied customers would yield an average of $26,854 in additional lifetime revenue, thereby underscoring the true value of these opinions.

How to Use Evaluation To Deliver Hospitable Healthcare

"What gets measured gets managed/done" is a fundamental principle

Tripp Welch, Vice Chair of Quality Management Services at the 150-year-old Mayo Clinic, explains their three-pronged approach that fuels word of mouth and generates over one million patients per year from every state and 147 countries.

"Much like the hospitality industry, we've used the Net Promoter Score to measure and track customer/patient satisfaction. But it's not sensitive enough for what we do, because our scores are so high. So, we focus on how many people check the very top box (patient satisfaction score) because that's a measure of trust.

The number one reason people come to the Mayo Clinic is our clinical expertise. Yet, what differentiates Mayo from every other healthcare organization is our teamwork and ability to work across multiple specialties and treat patients holistically. For example, it's not uncommon in our culture for a world expert in cardiovascular disease to pick up the phone and check with a colleague in neurology to see what he/she has to say about a specific patient. This is one of the principles on which the Mayo brothers founded Mayo Clinic . . .the way we operate brings a union of forces together in support of patients' needs."

of effective management. Measurements are not just used to hold employees accountable, but if similar to those mentioned in this chapter, they will help inform management about customers' attitudes, behaviors, and opinions about the service experience they received from your team. Measurements may also be used to evaluate the lifetime value (LTV) of customers. Some of the measurements we recommend healthcare providers use to evaluate the quality of service delivered include the following:

- Implement an ongoing program to solicit and review feedback from patients on the service they received within 24 hours of their visit. In addition to including questions about performance, ask patients to rate the relative *importance* of the performance features you are measuring.

- Distribute feedback survey forms electronically (via email or text) for ease of completion with the assurance that all responses will be treated as confidential. In addition, make sure your file of completed responses is representative of your patient census for each reporting period. For example, if 20% of your weekly patients interact with you and your team on Tuesdays, make sure your sample of respondents reflects a comparable percentage over the course of the week under review.

- Conduct sentiment analyses of postings about your hospital, clinic, or practice on social media to determine the polarity (positive or negative) of comments, discover service failures, and replicate these analyses in accord with a predetermined cadence.

CHAPTER 7

Reward: The *R* in PAEER

"People don't change their behavior unless it makes a difference for them to do so."

– SHARON STONE

Nothing Says "Thank You" Like a Reward

HEALTHCARE SERVICE PROVIDERS have considerable room for improvement in their quest to build patient loyalty, as evidenced by this enlightening observation: the average retention rate for patients treated by US hospital systems over the subsequent five-year period is a modest 43%.[1] Retention is defined as "repeated service encounters" of any kind by a provider with the same patient during the five-year term. By comparison, although the incidence of repeat patronage varies by the type of lodging—from economy to luxury—guests who were active members of US hotel loyalty programs in 2019 generated 56% of total revenue that year.[2] The multi-year percentage derived from guests enrolled in these programs was north of 60%.

The power of recognizing and rewarding customers for their patronage is evident in the omnipresence of programs designed to do so in practically every service industry. The genesis of these programs date to 1896 when the Sperry & Hutchinson Company introduced trading stamps. Their popularity gained traction in the 1960s as S&H expanded distribution through retailers such as grocery stores, gasoline stations and department stores, and enhanced the appeal of the products for which stamps could be redeemed.

Inspired by the success of the model in building customer loyalty, United Airlines first introduced a recognition program awarding customers plaques and other promotional materials in 1972 to capture and retain more repeat passengers for their otherwise perishable product: empty seats upon takeoff. American Airlines launched the first "modern" frequency program based on miles flown in 1981, and the rest, as they say, is history. Today, the 70-plus loyalty programs maintained by approximately 170 global airlines claim roughly 300,000,000 active members.[3] Enrollment in hotel loyalty programs is even more popular and continues to grow.

The appeal of loyalty programs to both product/service providers and consumers is clear. More than 90% of companies now offer some type of loyalty program,[4] and the majority (52%) of American consumers will join the loyalty program of a brand from which they make frequent purchases.[5]

Yet, such programs are conspicuously absent in healthcare. Among the few that exist, the benefits appear restricted to services designed to facilitate scheduling care but fail to categorize different cohorts of patients defined by their frequency of patronage, value to the enterprise, or what could arguably be considered motivational rewards.

There are several reasons for this. First, the belief that healthcare services are fundamentally different from the types of services for which loyalty programs are designed today— "need" versus "want" services—and therefore exempt from the otherwise acquisitive motivation that drives consumers' participation in such programs. This may be true for complex medical procedures such as coronary bypass surgery, but we believe it is less so for more commonplace procedures such as routine clinic visits, annual physicals, and so on.

Second, understandable concerns about ensuring such programs comply with prevailing governmental and/or other regulatory requirements, especially with respect to any financial inducements to encourage and reward repeat patronage. This is a reasonable concern yet fails to acknowledge the difference between recognition and reward, and their relative importance in such programs.

Third, the reticence that derives from the assumed complexity and cost associated with the introduction of such programs also looms as an obstacle. This concern should be weighed relative to the benefit of acquiring a greater share of the lifetime value of healthcare services required by patients, not just the short-term impact on profit and loss.

Finally, consideration should also be given to the apparent belief that such programs would denigrate the perceived quality or value of the healthcare services rendered. Again, this may be true for certain types of healthcare services, but not others. For example, programs that encourage the adoption of behaviors known to advance healthier lifestyles—exercise, good nutrition, sleep hygiene, medication compliance, screenings for potentially serious ailments, annual physicals, and so on—would be both reasonable and welcomed. Further, this objection presumes prospective program participants would have a diminished view of the value of the services provided, although their eagerness to enroll in such programs would reveal the veracity of this assumption.

The absence of loyalty programs in healthcare has perpetuated a very interesting and expensive present state: care is episodic. This, in turn, has led most healthcare service providers to invest marketing resources primarily in programs designed to acquire new patients, generally to the exclusion of funding programs designed to encourage and reward the loyalty of repeat patronage.

This myopia fails to acknowledge two important benefits of establishing an ongoing relationship with patients. First, sustained relationships with patients are likely to enhance their long-term well-being through observance of such things as preventative screenings, medication compliance, nutritional education, and wellness coaching. Second, curation of an ongoing relationship with patients will yield a favorable financial impact on the enterprise that derives from the capture of a greater share of their lifetime value. The latter is especially true given the increased cadence with which people seek and consume healthcare services as they age.

As reflected in our Gap Survey, satisfaction increases repeat patronage, and repeat patronage builds loyalty. Together, these relationships suggest healthcare service providers would be the beneficiaries of enhanced clinical and financial outcomes if they adopted relevant principles of hospitality to build patient loyalty. The fact that the majority (57%) of patients who seek care from a hospital system fail to return to the same system for care of any kind during the five years following their initial visit underscores the magnitude of this opportunity.

Importantly, from a clinical perspective, establishing a relationship with patients over multiple occasions of care for a variety of clinical services would advance providers' desire to improve the long-term well-being of the patients they serve. This would presumably be evidenced by patients' embrace of a healthier lifestyle, thereby reducing and/or eliminating certain costs associated with their need for future care. Loyalty programs that include appropriate rewards could also be introduced to facilitate this behavior.

Data from our Gap Survey reveal the stated likelihood of adults living a healthier lifestyle as a result of their participation in programs that include travel services and/or benefits as rewards for the desired behaviors assuming such programs existed: 62% for males, 60% for females. Capturing more of the lifetime value of care delivered to patients also represents a very attractive goal. The consultancy, PK Global, LLC, offers a compelling calculation of the magnitude of the financial opportunity lost when patients fail to continue to seek care from the same healthcare provider or system over time:[6]

- In 2021, the average (US) annual expenditure on healthcare per patient was $10,966.

- In 2021, the average (US) citizen was the age of 38, with an average life expectancy of 78 years.

- The aggregate expenditure for healthcare services over the future

40-year period until expected death was anticipated to be:

- $438,640, assuming no increase in the annual cost of healthcare services.
- $1,324,690, assuming a 5% annual increase in the cost of healthcare services.

The authors of the analysis underscore the significance of this lost opportunity for a family of four (assuming a 5% increase in annual cost) in an arresting conclusion: Retaining just 20 families would represent an average lifetime value contribution of $100 million to a care organization's top line.

Both the clinical and financial returns realized from loyal patients are palpable.

David Norton is Chairman of the creative media consultancy, GALE Partners. Prior to launching GALE, he spent 13 years as CMO of Harrah's & Caesar's Entertainment where he introduced Harrah's Total Rewards Program.

"Loyalty is the conduit between the customer and the business. There is a value proposition in loyalty: the customer gets recognition, rewards, and offers. In return, the business gets to understand who the customer is, their value and preferences."

Tailored For Healthcare

Assuming one accepts the premise that loyalty programs could enhance overall patient satisfaction in healthcare, it is important to define the components to ensure they address the important deficiencies revealed in our Gap research and comply with prevailing regulatory requirements. First, however, we need to clarify the difference between recognition and reward as both are critical components of successful loyalty programs.

Recognition is the practice of acknowledging and serving program participants in a manner that reflects their importance to the enterprise. *Importance* may be defined and classified in any of several ways: frequency of engagement, cumulative revenue realized from healthcare services provided, the cumulative margin realized from the same services, public advocacy beneficial to the institution, the reduced cost of future care attributable to the adoption of healthier lifestyles, and so on.

Although conferring the same degree of recognition on all participants might appear to be a laudable achievement, recognizing different cohorts of customers is an essential aspect of loyalty programs. This is for one very important reason stated previously: all customers are not created equal. Most customers understand recognition varies with their type and/or amount of consumption, and this determines their status in loyalty programs. They can

- stay more nights with the same hotel brand to receive complimentary upgrades;

- fly more often with the same airline to be eligible to check in at the "priority" counter;

- dine more frequently at the same restaurant to get access to preferred reservations; and

- purchase more items from the same retailer to receive bigger discounts.

As stated previously in chapter six, however, customer cohorts should be differentiated by how they are served, not how they are treated. For example, members of hospitality loyalty programs who check in at the main desk or counter receive the same gracious greeting and attentive service as those who check in at the "preferred" counter. Guests who dine at restaurants for which hard-to-get reservations are a prized possession enjoy the same cuisine and ambiance as those given VIP access. Shoppers who spend less with a specific retailer are offered the same tiered discounts as their more acquisitive colleagues and so forth.

This is an important distinction fundamental to the composition of hospitality loyalty programs: everyone is treated the same but served differently based on their status. This principle should be equally true with the creation and introduction of patient loyalty programs in healthcare: everyone should be treated with the same degree of care but may be served differently. For example, loyalty members may be given more choice in availability when scheduling appointments or endure shorter wait times in the clinic.

For healthcare organizations it is also important to underscore that recognition may be conferred without the express or implied financial benefit of reward.

Rewards are more tangible and accelerate engagement with loyalty programs. They also represent the currency that extends the duration of engagement with customers. Hospitality loyalty programs have traditionally used their own "currency" as rewards, such as free nights in the same hotel or chain, free tickets on the same or an affiliated airline, or free food and beverages in the host casino.

As these programs matured, however, it became increasingly clear that members wanted to use their accumulated currency to purchase other goods and services, for example: items from Home Depot, pizza from Domino's or office supplies from Office Depot. The most successful programs now permit redemption for non-sponsor products and services, and this flexibility of redemption has strengthened the loyalty of program participants as a result.

The application of this idea in healthcare is arguably more nuanced, however,

Jeff Arnold, Co-founder, Chairman, and Chief Executive Officer of Sharecare, a digital health company that helps people manage all their health in one place, explains the novel reward program his company introduced to major employers who are committed to advancing the well-being of their employees.

"The concept of a VSA—a Vacation Spending Account—that's embedded in our WeCare platform is the first of its kind in healthcare, based on our research and collective experience with reward programs to be an effective way to motivate behavior change. It can help the American worker navigate their well-being and make the healthy choice the easy choice while eliminating some of the barriers that prevent them from taking time to relax and recharge, which, in turn, will make employees not only healthier and happier people, but also productive."

because the US CMS, responsible for providing coverage to the roughly 35% of the population with healthcare insurance, proscribe the use of any remuneration by providers that directly encourages patients with government insurance to seek care from the conferring provider. Yet, the universal application of this policy is confounded by what is permissible in some states versus others, depending on differences in Medicare Advantage plan benefits and the applicable scope of benefits for Medicaid recipients. Further, the US Office of the Inspector General (OIG) published a final regulation of the Affordable Care Act in March 2017 announcing certain safe harbors for the use of incentives to attract patients that included guidelines for how such programs may be designed to avoid penalties under the federal civil monetary penalty (CMP) statute or anti-kickback statute (AKS).

Although the guidelines lack definitive clarity, they have been interpreted to suggest rewards that promote access to care (access to items and services that are payable by Medicare or a state health care program for the beneficiaries who receive them) are permissible so long as they pose a low risk of harm to the Medicare or Medicaid beneficiaries who receive them. As an example, providing Medicare or Medicaid recipients with free childcare to permit their attendance at a smoking cessation program would be permissible, while offering them free movie tickets to access the same program would not because the latter wouldn't remove a barrier to accessing the care. Bottom line: healthcare service providers may create and support loyalty programs that facilitate access to care within the guidelines established by OIG. Care must be exercised when composing the roster of rewards, however, and cash and/or items that may be converted to or used like cash is proscribed.

Yet, it is important to underscore the fact that restrictions imposed on the introduction of loyalty programs for patients with government insurance do not apply to the 65% of the insured population with private or commercial insurance. Hence, the curation of loyalty programs for these individuals is constrained only by management's creativity, judgment about the appropriateness of such rewards, the cost of program development and administration, patient receptivity, and the related optics. It is also reasonable to assume the economic value of reward programs in healthcare would accrue primarily to healthcare networks or systems that offer a wide array of services in multiple locations versus independent or individual healthcare service providers. This is because networked systems are better positioned to provide a more comprehensive roster of healthcare services to patients whose myriad of healthcare requirements evolve over time.

Frequency versus Loyalty

It is important to remind readers of the difference between frequency and loyalty, which was discussed briefly in chapter two. Customer loyalty derives from emotion, while customer frequency simply defines the cadence of purchase behavior.

To understand why loyalty programs are so important to hospitality service providers, it is first necessary to understand how the business model of the hospitality industry has changed over time. In the early years, hospitality service providers owned most of the physical assets (properties) they managed and the related operating businesses. This constrained their growth,

Adam Burke, who ran the Honors program at Hilton Corporation from 2004 to 2009, articulates this difference as follows:

"A frequency program focuses on the short-term win of using incentives to "buy the business." It is simply getting a particular incentive for a particular stay. A loyalty program, on the other hand, involves a much more holistic view of the customer. It recognizes that it's not a one-size-fits-all approach, lets the consumer define the most important elements of the relationship, and allows them the flexibility to alter those benefits with each individual interaction.

We'd like to know as much about our customers as they're willing to tell us. And with that, there is an incumbent responsibility to not only use that information responsibly, but also use it to further develop the relationship. If you start dating someone, they're not going to blame you if you don't know their birthday, their parents' names, their favorite color, etc. But if you're still forgetting birthdays several years later, the likelihood is you may not have a relationship anymore."

however, as they could only grow as fast as cash flow enabled them to purchase more properties.

In 1989, Marriott Corporation changed the model. They split the company into two separately traded organizations. One company, Marriott International, focused on franchising and managing hotels and resorts. The other company, Host Marriott, focused on owning hotels, resorts, and other physical assets. At the time they owned brands such as Bob's Big Boy Restaurants, Roy Rogers, an airline catering company, and the like. Host Marriott eventually sold many of these non-hotel assets.

This new operating strategy was dubbed *asset light* and is now the model embraced by most hospitality service providers, including hotels, restaurants, and some major casino companies such as MGM Resorts International. Asset light enabled these organizations to pursue less capital-intensive, more rapid growth.

In this asset light model, the service provider is a franchisor that allows another provider (franchisee) to license its brand name and either manage the asset themselves or have a third party manage the asset on their behalf. They may also have the franchisor manage the asset for them.

Because not all potential franchisees have the same access to expertise and capital, hospitality service providers created multiple brands that could be developed at different levels of investment and managed at different price points. For example, a franchisee with modest capital could franchise and build a Hampton Inn product from Hilton Corporation. A franchisee with access to more capital could franchise and build a Conrad product from Hilton. The greater the diversity of brands available to franchisees, the more opportunity there is for franchisors to grow their portfolio of service locations and, eventually, number of brand-loyal customers. The franchisee pays a fee to the franchisor for the privilege of using the franchisor's brand and must adhere to specific design and operating standards imposed by the franchisor. In return, the franchisor provides the necessary tools to help ensure the franchisee is successful by providing support for operations, marketing, purchasing, materials' management, and the like.

In recent years, franchisors have become more focused on brand management, as this ultimately determines the true value of their organization. The stronger the brand, the stronger market desire for the brand, from both a franchisee and customer perspective. This allows franchisors to grow their distribution network and build a larger customer base via more franchisees, thereby making the brand more valuable. For public companies, this typically translates into an increase in value as reflected in their stock price.

One reason there has been so much consolidation in the hospitality industry is that big providers buy smaller providers to access different brands and grow a wider distribution network. The other reason is that franchisors typically have high overhead costs in their corporate offices because of the many skilled professionals required to develop the brand, work with franchisees, market the brand, and so on. The more properties over which they can amortize these costs, the more profitable the franchisor can be.

What franchisors really provide, however, is access to a steady stream of customers who are loyal to the brand. These are customers with a demonstrated affinity for the brand who exhibit the positive behaviors of loyal customers. Hence, when choosing a franchisor with which to affiliate, franchisees typically evaluate which can supply the most loyal customers.

For franchisors to have a steady stream of customers, they must ensure those customers leave satisfied every time they visit a franchised location, otherwise they may switch to another brand and propagate negative word of mouth about the brand they abandoned. Service providers lose two valuable assets if or when this occurs: their reputation and their customers. Brands, therefore, are only as strong as their weakest franchisee. Franchisors must do everything possible to ensure a perfect customer experience every time and, if a visit goes bad, provide appropriate compensation for the aggrieved guest. You may recall this is what led Hampton Inn to offer a 100% satisfaction guarantee. To ensure a perfect visit, franchisors must not only know who the customers are, but their specific wants and needs as well. This information may then be passed to franchisees so they may ensure consistent delivery of the desired guest experience regardless of the service location.

Naturally, customers must identify themselves for franchisors to know their names, likes, and dislikes. How do hospitality service providers get customers do to this? Through the use of a quid pro quo: they entice customers to join the brand's loyalty program by rewarding them for their patronage, typically conferring some meaningful benefit every time they patronize a branded location. These typically include bonus reward program points, free Wi-Fi, a reduced nightly rate, and so on.

Of course, once customers have enrolled in a frequency program, it is then up to the provider to use the information it collects on their habits and preferences to create an emotional bond with the brand. We discuss how hospitality service providers accomplish this next.

We believe some form of this asset light/franchised brand model will be embraced by healthcare service providers who have strong brands and are eager to grow without committing significant amounts of development capital.

Customer Loyalty in the Hospitality Industry

Two seminal articles, one published in the *Cornell Hotel and Restaurant Administration Quarterly*[7] and the other, a case study on Hilton's Honors program published by Harvard Business School,[8] illuminate the antecedents and consequences of customer loyalty and corresponding financial value of loyal customers to hospitality brands. The Cornell Quarterly article revealed that customer reward programs, such as those developed by S&H Green Stamps, airlines, and hotel companies, are very effective at creating frequency, but they alone do not create the emotional bond necessary to build true loyalty. Without this bond, research has shown customers are inclined to switch brands when they believe another offers a better deal.

The Harvard case illustrated how the Honors program enabled Hilton to increase systemwide occupancy to a profitable level (typically above 62%). Without the program, management calculated annual occupancy would have been below the 62% threshold (we discuss metrics to measure loyalty later in the chapter). Even though these analyses were undertaken several years ago, similar results have been observed in numerous similar analyses conducted since then.

Loyalty programs have also become highly valuable balance sheet assets of hospitality brands, as evidenced by their significant valuation in the recent COVID-related debt financing raised by such organizations as Delta Airlines and Hilton Hotels.

One of the constructs to emerge from the research presented in the *Cornell Quarterly* by Bowen and Shoemaker was the Model of Service Relationships, which is shown in Figure 7.1. This model illustrates the antecedents and consequences of commitment in service relationships.

Figure 7.1: A model of service relationships.

One significant metric of loyalty is *relationship commitment*, shown at the bottom of the model with the arrows pointing toward it. Relationship commitment is the belief that an ongoing relationship is so important that both the service provider and customer are willing to work at maintaining it, and willing to make short-term sacrifices to realize long-term benefits.

The consequences of relationship commitment include increased product usage such as frequenting a restaurant versus dining elsewhere and voluntary activities that one partner is likely to undertake on behalf of the other. These might include actions such as spreading positive word of mouth or actively making business referrals. Note, the preceding are all positive outcomes of commitment. Negative outcomes result from lack of commitment.

We found clear evidence of commitment (loyalty) in our Gap Survey. As shown in Figure 7.2, the percentage of respondents claiming loyalty to hospitality service providers, both hotels and restaurants, is significantly higher than for those claiming loyalty to hospitals or walk-in clinics.

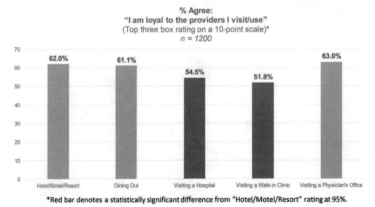

Figure 7.2: Customer loyalty to service providers.

One of the constructs that leads to commitment or loyalty is *trust*. Trust is the belief that an individual or exchange partner may be relied upon to keep his or her word and promise. Trust is an antecedent of loyalty because customers trust organizations to do the things they are supposed to do, implicitly or explicitly. It is important to note that opportunistic behavior will typically result in a lack of trust. This means service providers cannot arbitrarily take advantage of customers, especially their best customers. If they do, they violate customers' trust in them. When customers have trust, there is a greater likelihood they will also display commitment. The opposite is also true.

Another construct that leads to commitment is *value*. This is much more than a financial construct. Value includes temporal or time saving, functional, emotional, social, trust, and episodic components.

Certainty, knowing that the service provider does what it says it will, is yet another construct that leads to commitment.

Benefits are also important. This construct refers to things hospitality service providers give only to customers whose purchase behavior has enabled them to achieve a certain status. Typically, these benefits are not available to guests who exhibit lower levels of spending. Examples of benefits conferred by hospitality service providers include:

- Members of hotel loyalty programs are exempted from time-consuming registration formalities.
- Hotels provide complimentary room upgrades to loyal customers.
- Frequent hotel guests may check in and out at times that suit them.
- Hotels customize the amenities and services guests desire each stay based on their historical preferences.
- Restaurants reserve their best tables for loyal customers.
- Airlines permit frequent flyers to select the best seats, board first, and access highly coveted overhead bin space.
- Casinos allow preferred guests to register in private lounges stocked with complimentary food and beverages.
- For all providers, employees acknowledge your problems are important to them and address them on the spot.

What other actions create trust in, and loyalty toward, hospitality service providers? As Adam Burke, former Senior Vice President of Hilton Hotels responsible for their Honors loyalty program, mentioned in a conversation with Shoemaker:

It's not just a smile, points/miles, whether you get a room upgrade, or additional amenities. It's a host of other things such as how we communicate with you (how often and the types of information sent), how you want to earn the currency and how you want to redeem that currency. So, if you're going to develop true loyalty, it must be on the customer's terms, not yours.

Figure 7.3 from our Gap Survey also reveals hospitality service providers are more likely to try and satisfy guests with the services they receive than healthcare service providers. This underscores one of the consequences of healthcare service providers delivering poor service: namely, a lack of commitment or loyalty, evident across all three categories.

Unhappy customers visiting hospitality service providers are more likely to switch than customers who are unhappy with healthcare service providers, however. This is because of the ease with which consumers can source and engage alternative hospitality service providers versus alternative healthcare providers as noted previously. The willingness of customers to quickly default to other hospitality service providers is why so many providers have invested significant resources in cultivating the loyalty of their customers.

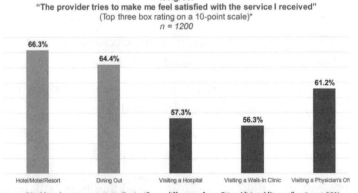

% Agree:
"The provider tries to make me feel satisfied with the service I received"
(Top three box rating on a 10-point scale)*
n = 1200

*Red bar denotes a statistically significant difference from "Hotel/Motel/Resort" rating at 95%.

Figure 7.3: Service provider efforts to enhance customer satisfaction.

The Hilton Honors case study also addressed the financial impact of customer loyalty on Hilton Worldwide. Table 7.1 illustrates the pro forma financial impact of the program for a sample hotel on a nightly basis. (Note: These data are for illustrative purposes only and do not reflect actual performance.)

Without the loyalty program, projected occupancy in the hotel would be 86%. However, with the additional guests attracted because of the loyalty program it would be 90%. The four-percentage point difference would yield $1,417.50 in additional daily revenue. This is room revenue only and does not account for the fact that loyal members also spend more money on the property for other services than non-loyal members, thereby delivering additional revenue. The cost of generating this additional $1,417.50 in revenue is only $318.94, thereby yielding a nightly return on the investment to the owner of 344.4%.

Column	NEEDED INFORMATION	
A	B	C
2	Number of rooms	200
3	Room rate	$175
4	On given night percentage of people staying in hotel who are members of the loyalty program	22.50%
5	Percentage who stay in hotel solely because of the program	20%
6	Incremental stay (C4*C5)	4.5%
7	Total rooms sold	180
8	Room revenue (C7*C3)	$31,500.00
9	Program revenue (C8*C4)	$7,987.50
10	Incremental revenue (C8*C9)	$1,417.50
11	Revenue of those come anyway (1-C6)*C8	$30,082.50
13	Total occupancy percentage with the program (C7/C2)	90.0%
14	Incremental rooms sold (C7*C6)	8
15	Check to see if (C14*C3)=C10	$1,417.50
16	Total occupancy percentage without the program (C7-C14)/C2	85.95%
Column A	COST TO OWNER	
2	Point cost per $1 revenue	$0.045
3	Program revenue (C9)	$7,087.50
4	COST - owner pays brand (C20*C19)	$318.94
5	Incremental revenue (C10)	$1,417.50
6	ROI (C22-C21)/C21	344.4%

Table 7.1: Pro forma impact of customer loyalty at a sample Hilton hotel.

Josh Margolis is Vice President of Customer Journey for Caesars Entertainment where he leads a team of customer experience and product development professionals.

"Effective loyalty programs are those that anticipate what customers want and satisfy their desires. The easier the customer journey, the better. To build loyalty, healthcare providers should avoid asking returning patients information they already collected. And the person who has a recurring condition and goes to the same doctor once or twice a month should be treated differently than the person who goes there once a year.

The deal in loyalty programs is simple: the customer gets something, and the company gets the customer's data. Businesses need feedback through data to build loyalty at scale, and this feedback may then be used to create personalized experiences."

It is worth noting that the private equity firm, Blackstone, bought Hilton for $26 billon in an all-cash deal in 2007, took Hilton public in 2013, sold its shares in 2018, and realized a cumulative net profit of over $14 billion in the 11 years it owned Hilton. Hilton's Honors program was a significant contributor to the company's evolved value.[9]

From Frequency to Loyalty

Figure 7.4 illustrates how hospitality service provider frequency programs have matured to build long-term customer loyalty over time. The journey to loyalty began when service providers started using the data collected to improve the customer experience. This occurred in frequency programs at the 4.0 stage. At 5.0, data collected from other sources, such as customer's social media accounts and data mining services, were merged with the service provider's data to develop a 360-degree profile of guests. The related insights are used to create positive experiences for those guests. The information is also used to protect guests from the consequences of service failures.

Notice that early models of frequency programs were more tactical and did not increase the profitability of the host providers as much as later versions. As frequency programs matured to become more strategic loyalty programs through the data collected to help improve the customer experience, the host service providers became even more profitable.

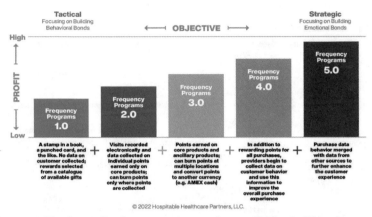

Figure 7.4: How hospitality frequency programs have evolved to build loyalty.

Figure 7.4 illustrates the steps required to evolve from frequency (version 1.0) to loyalty (version 5.0). One column of the table focuses on service variables critical to hospitality service providers, and a second column illustrates how Hilton—whose loyalty program was rated number one in the hotel industry in 2020 by The Points Guy[10]—incorporates some of these elements in its honors program. The same features would apply to patient loyalty programs developed by healthcare service providers.

Table 7.2 provides an overview of the architecture of the Hilton Honors loyalty program. *(See next page)*

Implications for Healthcare Organizations

The market dynamics that have made reward programs a fundamental and highly effective component of the contemporary business model embraced by the most successful hospitality service providers include:

- intense competition for new customers;
- greater focus on nurturing new customers to become loyal customers;
- more knowledgeable and demanding customers inclined to switch to alternative brands if they have a poor experience;

FEATURE	IN HILTON HONORS
A robust database that provides a 360-degree view of the customer behavior	123 million members; tracks all purchases, comments, and the like
Build a wide network so there are many opportunities for customers to earn and redeem rewards	18 brands, 6,700 properties with 1.02 million rooms in 122 countries
Targeted communications to customers on their terms	Customers tell Hilton what they want to hear and how often
Meaningful rewards from customers' perspective, not Hilton's	Can redeem points for free nights, purchases on Amazon, exclusive experiences, charitable contributions; ability to pool points
Simplicity: easy for customers to enroll, understand and use	Offers a flexible payment slider that lets members choose any combination of points and miles to book a stay
Motivational rewards that are attainable	Offers co-branded credit card with American Express so members can add points multiple ways
Measurability to ensure the program is yielding the intended outcomes, changing behavior	Data presented in table 7.1 illustrate measurability
Value of benefits based on their worth to customers Value of benefits based on their worth to customers	Four membership tiers are available to members based on the number of nights they stay each year in Hilton branded properties: (1) Member (0-6 nights), (2) Silver (7+nights), (3) Gold (28+nights), (4) Diamond (42+nights)
Franchisee compliance endorsement and support	Properties have an employee whose responsibility is to take care of Hilton Honors members; there are individual property contests held to enroll members

Table 7.2: Hilton Honors loyalty program profile.

- industry consolidation with service providers owning, operating, or franchising multiple brands;

- aggressive franchising of brands to grow the geographic footprint of service locations;

- rigorous enforcement of brand standards across the service network to ensure common customer experiences;

- regional and national brand communications that establish and/ or reinforce consistent brand standards; and

- "gamification" of customer mentality, resulting in a quid pro quo to encourage repeat patronage.

How to Reward Patients To Deliver Hospitable Healthcare

One of the most provocative recommendations presented in this chapter is to explore the introduction of a program that recognizes and rewards patients based on the frequency—and value—of their patronage. Commonplace procedures such as blood tests and vaccinations are well-suited for such recognition programs because they encourage patients to visit the same service provider when these services are required instead of visiting a different provider. The rewards could include privileged or complimentary access to future services and/or programming designed to enhance the well-being of recipients. And because the focus of these programs would be on recognizing versus rewarding patients, they could be developed and managed in a manner compliant with prevailing regulatory requirements. Given the demonstrated power of these programs in the hospitality industry, we recommend healthcare service providers do the following:

1. Invest in a CRM program that builds and updates patient profiles inclusive of personal preference information to enable enhanced recognition for patients who visit more frequently.

2. Ensure patients are personally thanked for their patronage prior to departure, then follow this with an email or text expression of thanks within 24 hours.

3. Invite patients to join a hospital/practice-specific "patient appreciation club" that rewards them for their patronage with privileged access to complimentary health screenings, lectures, demonstrations, and other incentives that would enhance their well-being.

The same market forces that reshaped the hospitality industry are reinventing healthcare today. Hence, we believe healthcare service providers will soon acknowledge the wisdom of introducing recognition and reward programs to minimize the exodus of patients to competitive providers and capture the lifetime value of the patients they serve. We discuss lifetime value and other metrics that may be used by healthcare service providers to evaluate the merits of introducing principles of hospitality in the next chapter.

CHAPTER 8

The ROI

"One accurate measurement is worth a thousand expert opinions."

– GRACE HOPPER

The Bottom Line

IN THE PREVIOUS CHAPTERS, WE introduced the five components of the PAEER model. In this chapter, we consider what has become a vitally important driver of both growth and loyalty in the hospitality industry and its possible application to healthcare: the practice of recognizing and rewarding customers for their patronage.

At first, the idea of rewarding patients for their patronage and subsequent loyalty to a healthcare provider might seem inappropriate or even illegal if inappropriate incentives are used. Yet hospitality service customers have come to expect providers will recognize their patronage in ways that acknowledge their value and thus establish lasting relationships. The motivation for providers is obvious: it costs far less to nurture an ongoing relationship with a satisfied customer than to source and convert a new one. The economics of establishing lifetime relationships with customers are compelling too.

We discuss how best to calculate the return on investment required to apply rewards. As stated so astutely in the introductory quote from Grace Hopper, objective measurement should determine the latter, not the opinions of "experts."

So, we now introduce the last component of the PAEER model: *R for Reward.*

Defining ROI

Calculating the return on investment (ROI) is relatively straightforward when the independent variables (components of cost) and dependent variables (desired outcomes observed within some defined period) are objective and quantifiable. This is less true when the dependent variables are surrogates for the desired outcome at some future date. Examples of the latter include such things as higher brand awareness, enhanced brand image, or improvements in guest/patient satisfaction, as predictors of loyalty. This is because there are many catalysts of brand choice including availability, access restrictions, price, and competitive alternatives. This is true for both hospitality and healthcare service providers.

Nevertheless, investments designed to enhance the overall customer experience must be evaluated by predictive metrics and also, with respect to some reasonable cadence, to estimate both their short-term and enduring impact on organizational performance. This evaluation is essential to determine the wisdom of sustaining, amending, or terminating the related investments to achieve a desired return over time.

The Independent Variables

Because the greatest opportunity to improve patient satisfaction lies in the adoption of service strategies imported from the hospitality industry, much of the required expense of implementation already flows through the profit and loss statements of healthcare service providers. This includes the cost of recruiting, training, compensating, and rewarding staff, plus system-related costs for such things as database development, data processing and IT support. Additional investment may be required for public area or clinic facility servicescape design and furnishing, software upgrades or replacements and, if adopted, the development and maintenance of a patient loyalty program. Yet, these expenses may be amortized over the years in which the enterprise benefits from the expected increase in patient satisfaction and the related revenue.

All of these expenses should be considered with reference to the financial health of the enterprise and, importantly, a realistic assessment of the incremental income the enterprise would realize by making the required investments. Further, required investments may also be phased over a reasonable period during which the host provider acclimates to implementation of the newly adopted service strategies.

The Dependent Variables

The ROI that derives from improvement in the overall patient experience should be evaluated with reference to five dependent variables:

1. The sentiment expressed in patient-authored communications about the provider.
2. The provider's reputation among key constituents including existing patients, prospective patients, the public, the clinical community, and payors, both offline and online.
3. The incidence and trending of patient satisfaction.
4. The incidence and trending of repeat patronage and patient loyalty.
5. The related revenue/financial results.

The volume of patient-authored communications about providers has exploded as a direct result of patients' rapid engagement with social media. Patients are far more likely than ever before to share their experiences with, and opinions about, healthcare service providers through the digital megaphone of the internet. As revealed in our Gap Survey, and previously in Figure 6.1, more the one-third of adults review comments on social media about providers they are planning to use. Providers are therefore encouraged to monitor the sentiment of commentary posted about them on provider review/rating websites, community bulletin boards, and other widely available sources of patient-authored opinions. These insights should supplement the feedback that is solicited and received directly from patients, as was advocated in chapter six.

The incidence of consumers sharing information about their experiences with providers they visit/use was also revealed previously in chapter six but merits re-stating here. Specifically, as revealed in Figure 6.8, most respondents in our Gap Survey acknowledged engaging in this behavior across all categories measured with the highest incidence in healthcare noted for telling friends and family about experiences with physicians.

And as shown in chapter two, most consumers are also inclined to express dissatisfaction if they receive unsatisfactory service. One-third enlist social media to broadcast this discontent in addition to sharing comments by word of mouth.

Periodic measurement of a provider's reputation among key constituents is therefore recommended. Although their relative importance to the enterprise may vary by healthcare provider, these constituents include patients, both existing and prospective; members of the clinical and payor communities whose opinions or referrals impact the provider; and the public.

Various methodologies for the measurement of brand quality and reputation have evolved in recent years, yet these typically include an analysis of information in the public domain plus opinions expressed in proprietary research. Some results appear in survey reports published by a variety of organizations. In the hospitality industry, these include *U.S. News & World Report, Forbes Travel Guide, JD Power, AAA Guide, Travel + Leisure,* and *Consumer Reports.* In the healthcare industry, these include *U.S. News & World Report, Healthgrades, WebMD, CMS Care Compare, LeapFrogGroup,* and *YouGov.*

Once providers have decided on the appropriate methodology

and metrics, however, it is important to replicate the analysis in accord with a specific cadence to observe any changes in perceived quality or reputation over time and address emerging deficiencies before they become endemic.

The incidence of patient satisfaction associated with repeat patronage should also be evaluated as a dependent variable because it is the precursor of brand loyalty. Recall that frequency of patronage should not be confused with loyalty, however. The former is simply the number of times a consumer patronizes a service provider, perhaps as a matter of convenience or, in the case of healthcare, because the provider is "in network" and the financial implications of using an out-of-network provider are deemed prohibitive. Loyalty, however, exists when a consumer elects to patronize a service provider because of the emotional bond that has been created between the consumer and the brand. It exists when a consumer selects the same brand over the majority of repeated purchase cycles (from purchase to consumption, then repurchase) and does so even when acceptable substitutes are readily available.

The last dependent variable that should be factored into the calculation of ROI is perhaps the most obvious: the related revenue and financial results. This should be calculated on an annual basis, yet we believe evaluating the financial ROI over both the near and long-term provides a more appropriate frame of reference. This is because the positive impact of many hospitality service initiatives may not manifest in immediate or short-term financial results.

The importance of building loyalty among customers, both guests in hospitality and patients in healthcare, is underscored by another observation revealed in our Gap Survey: how unsatisfactory service impacts repeat patronage. As shared previously, most consumers do not return to providers from whom they receive unsatisfactory service. This behavior is more pronounced as it relates to hotels, resorts, and restaurants, but it also applies to each of the three categories of healthcare service providers: visiting a hospital, walk-in clinic, and physician's office. Clearly, the negative implication for ROI over the full term of a guest's or patient's patronage is significant.

Lifetime Value

The lifetime value of a customer is defined as the theoretical value of a customer over the full term of his or her purchase and consumption of the same or similar services. Capturing customers' continued visitation and spending habits is the holy grail for many service marketers. Only a modest investment is required to build and sustain loyalty versus the more significant investment required to source and convert a continuous supply of new customers. There is also an intangible benefit associated with customer loyalty: the positive communications they express or publish about the providers they patronize, and the incremental revenue providers derive from these unsolicited endorsements.

Calculating the lifetime value of patients is a relatively new undertaking for many healthcare service providers because the prevailing business model for most is based on episodic care. Patients present, are treated, billed, and then, for the most part, forgotten until or unless they present once again. Further, the lifetime value of patients varies by several factors including their age, gender, relative health, nature of the illness(es) for which they seek treatment, insurance coverage, and point of origin, an especially important factor for healthcare service providers who attract international patients.

These differences should be borne in mind when calculating lifetime value.

Lifetime Value in the Healthcare Industry

One very important benefit healthcare service providers realize from earning the loyalty of patients is the positive impact their continuing patronage has on enterprise revenue and, hopefully, margin.

This scenario is one in which initial encounters for episodic care morph into an extended relationship for either chronic or lifetime care—where disparate healthcare services provided to the same patient over multiple years or to members of the patient's family—without the provider having to incur the marketing expense to replace the lost revenue due to patient attrition.

The related ROI may be quantified by calculating the lifetime value (LTV) of the relationship. In its most basic form, this is the product of the expected average visits per year (AVY) by the average net billing value per visit (ANBV) and the number of years (NY) over which the visits will occur:

$$LTV = (AVY) \times (ANBV) \times (NY)$$

For example, assume a patient makes an average of two visits to a provider per year from which the provider earns an average net billing value of $125 for a period of 23 years. The corresponding lifetime value of this patient would be $(2) \times (\$125) \times (23) = \$5,750$.

More sophisticated and actionable analyses of lifetime value derive from calculations that contemplate additional factors including:

- the average net margin per visit (versus net billing value), which varies by the service provided. This metric adjusts the lifetime value to reflect the direct cost of delivering the care plus any related marketing and/or other administrative expenses;

- the lifetime value for each cohort of patients (e.g., patients receiving cardiac versus pediatric care, etc.) to determine the weighted average of either the net billing value or net margin for the population of all patients served over the term of the analysis;

- a factor that reflects any expected degradation in loyalty over time, such as the average number of visits expressed as a percentage of total annual healthcare visits because of competitive, logistic, or other reasons; and

- a factor that reflects the incremental value of new patients earned on referrals from loyal patients without incurring additional marketing expense to attract those patients.

Amending the calculation of lifetime value through these adjustments will provide a much more accurate estimate of the ROI realized from the investment made in programs that build patient loyalty.

Ideally, the ROI of the total investment made to enhance the patient experience should be evaluated using both qualitative and quantitative metrics. The former include changes in the surrogate measures that predict repeat patronage over time, such as patient satisfaction, brand awareness, and brand image. The latter include financial results, such as revenue or margin, deemed directly attributable to the investment over a defined period of time. The financial ROI of the total investment may be calculated once the method of estimating lifetime value has been decided. This is typically expressed as a ratio of the lifetime value to the investment in either present or future dollars. The resulting percentage is then evaluated by management to determine its sufficiency relative to other possible uses of the funds invested.

Although the financial ROI that derives from patient loyalty applies to all healthcare service providers, it is especially significant for hospital systems and/or healthcare service provider networks that offer a broad array of healthcare services to patients in different geographic locations over their lifetime of care. Such an array increases the probability of capturing visits associated with the required care and decreases the likelihood of patients seeking care from providers who are not part of the system or network.

Lifetime Value in Hospitality

Hospitality service providers calculate the lifetime value of customers slightly differently and typically examine spending rate, retention rate, variable costs, and discount rate to compute net present value, or the value of future dollars in today's dollars. These calculations reveal that the lifetime value of a customer increases as the number of customer defections decreases and customer retention increases. The opposite is also true. Namely, as the number of customer defections increases, the lifetime value of a customer decreases. This is illustrated in Tables 8.1 and 8.2.

As reflected in the tables, during the first year, the profit per customer in both tables is equal to $81.40. Table 8.1 reveals what happens to the lifetime value when defections decrease (illustrating higher retention) while Table 8.2 reveals what happens to the lifetime value when defections increase (illustrating lower retention). Notice in Table 8.1, the lifetime value in year two is $136.91 and in Table 8.2, it is $125.50. For year three, these numbers are $176.56 and $147.44, respectively.

	YEAR 1	YEAR 2	YEAR 3
Customers	5,000	3,650	2,884
Retention Rate	73% (3650/5000)	79%	NA
Spending Rate	$148	$159	$165
TOTAL REVENUE	$740,000 ($148*5000)	$580,350	$475,860
Variable Costs %	45%	45%	45%
Variable Costs ($)	$333,000 ($740,000*.45)	$261,158	$214,137
GROSS PROFIT	$407,000 (740K-333K)	$319,193	$261,723
Discount Rate (15%)	1	1.15	1.32
NPV Profit	$407,000	$277,559 [($319,193)/(1+.15)^1]	$198,275 ($261,723/1.32)
Cumulative NPV Profit	407,000	$684,559	$882,834
LIFETIME VALUE	$81.40 ($407,000/5000)	$136.91 ($684,559/5000)	$176.56 ($882,834/5000)

Table 8.1: Customer lifetime value when defections decrease.

When calculating lifetime value, one should always divide the cumulative net present value profit by the number of customers at the beginning of the term of analysis. Note, this was 5,000 in Tables 8.1

	YEAR 1	YEAR 2	YEAR 3
Customers	5,000	3,650	2,884
Retention Rate	73% (3650/5000)	79%	NA
Spending Rate	$148	$159	$165
TOTAL REVENUE	$740,000 ($148*5000)	$580,350	$475,860
Variable Costs %	45%	45%	45%
Variable Costs ($)	$333,000 ($740,000*.45)	$261,158	$214,137
GROSS PROFIT	$407,000 (740K-333K)	$319,193	$261,723
Discount Rate (15%)	1	1.15	1.32
NPV Profit	$407,000	$277,559 [($319,193)/(1+.15)^1]	$198,275 ($261,723/1.32)
Cumulative NPV Profit	407,000	$684,559	$882,834
LIFETIME VALUE	$81.40 ($407,000/5000)	$136.91 ($684,559/5000)	$176.56 ($882,834/5000)

Table 8.2: Customer lifetime value when defections increase.

and 8.2. This is because one never knows which of the 5,000 initial customers will become loyal. To project the value of current customers in future dollars (assuming they continue to patronize the service provider), the calculation should include this number of customers in the denominator.

Implications for Healthcare

So, how may healthcare service providers use this information in their organization? We suggest three ways to go about it:

1. The lifetime value estimate helps management understand how much money to invest in a patient. For instance, if a service failure costs $500 to fix, management should fix it if the lifetime value of the patient is estimated to yield an attractive multiple of $500 over the expected term of future patronage.

2. If one looks at the lifetime value of different cohorts of patients, as

recommended above, the service provider can easily determine which are more versus less profitable. This insight would help management optimize the mix of patients served to the extent possible.

3. Although less applicable to healthcare today and more likely in the future, the lifetime value analysis may be used when evaluating the performance of a promotion or other marketing actions. Typically, the success of a promotion is determined based on the current revenue generated less the cost of the promotion. Yet, the fallacy of this type of analysis is that it does not account for the lifetime value of new patients who materialize specifically because of the promotion and become loyal.

Given the multiple determinants of patient satisfaction, the ROI calculated on investments made to enhance the patient experience should incorporate both observed changes in the surrogate measures likely to have a favorable impact on revenue over time and the related financial return. Further, the results should be evaluated over both the near (annual) and long (multi-year) term. The market impact of improvements in brand awareness and reputation occurs over multiple years and is subject to variation based on such things as patients' media habits and competitors' market presence and aggressiveness.

Specific ROI milestones should also be established prior to funding the development and activation of service strategies to determine the sufficiency of observed returns and the destiny of related programs. These should include acceptable targets for the financial return on invested capital, plus the intangible predictors of future consumer behavior that derive from consumers' impressions of, and intentions toward, the provider brand.

Now we offer some concluding thoughts on the path toward hospitable healthcare.

CHAPTER 9

Toward Hospitable Healthcare

"The world as we have created it is a process of our thinking. It cannot be changed without changing our thinking."

– ALBERT EINSTEIN

THE QUOTE ABOVE ADDRESSES THE enemy of change we believe many healthcare organizations will face as they implement the principles examined in this book. Yet, meaningful change does not require radical revisions to policy or operating standards. Rather, it may be achieved simply by taking incremental and disciplined steps toward the desired goal.

The Gap Survey research presented throughout this book reveals where healthcare service providers could benefit from adoption of the principles developed and refined by hospitality service providers. Their past 50 years of research, trial, and continuous refinement in practice provide important clues as to how similar results may be achieved in healthcare.

The market dynamics that led the hospitality industry to develop customer-centric service strategies were introduced in chapter one (Figure 1.4). We believe similar market dynamics are transforming the healthcare industry today, as reflected in Figure 9.1.

This figure reveals how healthcare is moving from a fragmented state with providers focused on caring solely for the patients they serve in their local or regional markets, to a more inclusive state. Providers are beginning to serve a greater census of patients in larger networks

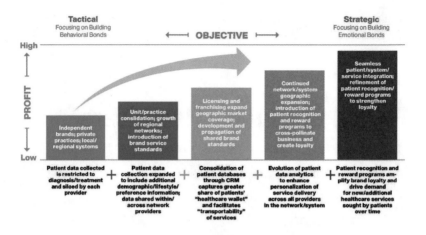

Figure 9.1: Data drivers of healthcare provider/system evolution.

created through affiliations, shared ownership, licensing, and franchising. These networks will provide welcomed integration between the system, patients, and services they receive.

An example of this type of network exists at the University of Texas MD Anderson Cancer Center with its expanded footprint across the US and internationally through partner, certified, and associate network members offering the "MD Anderson approach to cancer."[1] A similar goal inspired the recent acquisition of Cancer Treatment Centers of America Global, Inc. by City of Hope to create one of the largest cancer care networks in the US.[2]

Brand strength is not the only benefit of this type of network growth. A 2019 study by Deloitte revealed how the growth of physician networks can help bring down the cost of healthcare and improve patient satisfaction.[3] Another study undertaken in June 2021 by the healthcare research firm, Aberdeen, consisted of interviews conducted with executives from hospitals, physicians' offices, nursing homes, assisted living facilities, laboratories, and other clinics. Aberdeen surveyed 1,357 such organizations to understand the most pressing issues facing their front-line staff employed in admissions, nursing, billing, and the like.[4] "Keeping up with changes in customer needs and business conditions," topped the list. The results suggest the healthcare industry currently occupies a similar point in time to that when Kemmons Wilson took his legendary trip from Memphis to Washington, DC and revolutionized the hospitality industry.

As Mr. Wilson grew Holiday Inn and other hospitality brands began to develop, issues such as the lack of orchestration between enterprise systems used in service and back of the house activities also began to emerge as disparate property owners maintained different operating systems. This led hospitality service providers to standardize these systems and profile guests across several different aspects of purchase as they matured their loyalty programs.

Of course, the introduction of loyalty programs was just one of the many strategies the hospitality industry introduced over the years to achieve superior customer satisfaction scores. Our PAEER model derives from these strategies. Recall that the model provides a blueprint to reimagine healthcare service delivery and illustrates how implementation of the service strategies associated with each of the five components will enhance the patient experience: *P* for Prepare, *A* for Anticipate, the first *E* for Engage, the second *E* for Evaluate, and *R* for Reward. Yet, healthcare service providers must execute each component of the

Laurence Geller, an acclaimed hotelier and philanthropist, is Chairman of Geller Capital Partners and founder of LoveDay, a growing network of residential facilities in the UK that treat patients suffering from dementia. LoveDay integrates principles of hospitality with a commitment to clinical excellence in compassionate settings. Each facility features programming that reflects the needs of individual patients in accommodations that reflect the design and service standards found in Five-Star hotels and resorts.

"Our corporate ethos is reflected in a simple but compelling mantra: 'Above and Beyond.' This is our resolute commitment to be the very best in everything we do for the audiences we serve: residents, their families and loved ones, and our team members who provide the compassionate care. It is reflected in the interior design and furnishing of our residences, the quality of the cuisine we serve, the beneficial therapies we develop for each resident, and the exceptionally attentive care they receive."

Laurence Geller CONT.

"It reflects our commitment to do whatever is necessary to extend the lives of our residents in a dignified manner.

The patients we serve enjoy both quality and length of life that exceed the national norms by a significant measure. We believe this is a direct result of the comprehensive assessment we conduct of prospective residents . . . including their clinical requirements, present home environment and active life before dementia . . . to develop bespoke programming that enhances their physical, psychological, and social well-being. And we provide this programming in luxury accommodations we operate at a Five-Star service standard.

We naturally evaluate the professional qualifications of every prospective staff member when assessing their appropriateness to join our team, but the most important consideration is how they fare on our empathy quotient. This is a measure of their likelihood of delivering the exceptional level of hospitality we provide to our patients."

model well to enhance the overall patient experience. They must think and act holistically, focusing on all components, not just one.

Converging Forces

As stated at the beginning of this book, three converging trends underscore the exigent need for healthcare service providers to adopt many service strategies refined by their colleagues in the hospitality industry: (1) the new "information everywhere" environment that has precipitated more patient-directed selection of healthcare service providers; (2) advocacy for more transparent pricing of healthcare services to enable greater competition and more informed consumer choice; and (3) the fact that most healthcare providers must now engage in direct-to-consumer marketing to attract new patients. Each of these three points has gained considerable momentum in recent years, and the implications for how healthcare service providers must evolve their approach to understanding, recognizing, engaging, and rewarding patients for their patronage are profound.

ONLINE REVIEWS

The "information everywhere" phenomenon will exert even greater influence on patients' selection of healthcare service providers as they feel more comfortable posting, accessing, reviewing, and acting upon the growing crescendo of information about their healthcare service providers and experiences. According to a survey conducted by Dr. Jeffrey Kullgren of the University of Michigan, fully four out of ten adults over 50 years of age rely on online reviews before making an appointment with a physician.[5]

This incidence will undoubtedly increase in the years ahead and spawn the introduction of new and increasingly siloed service provider rating services by institution, specialty, and so on. Unfortunately, some of these will likely be inspired more by commercial interests than a genuine commitment content objectivity. This, in turn, will require providers to invest in more diligent policing of ratings and other critical information posted online to identify and address specious information that could misinform patients or even harm them.

The resources required of healthcare service providers to ensure this level of scrutiny will clearly surpass those most have committed to managing their online presence and social media to date.

EASIER ACCESS TO CARE

The evolution and rapid adoption of technology across the arc of healthcare will facilitate easier access to care through

Horst Schulze, legendary hotelier and former CEO/ Founder of the Ritz Carlton Hotel Company and Capella Hotel Group, is wont to say, "Culture eats strategy for breakfast." Focusing on people, systems, and service, he describes how he created cultures in which guests felt special and good about themselves.

"We didn't hire employees to work for us; we selected them to join our mission and vision of creating excellence in what we did. I wanted them to feel respected by both the market and customer.

Most companies do a lousy job training their new employees. Many turn over a new employee to another employee on the first day, and that employee then tells the new employee, "This company sucks." That's their orientation. How can you expect anything good to come of that? We made sure our employees knew what they could expect from us on their first day of work. We introduced them to our vision and our purpose: to be respected as the nicest people in the hotel business in the world. That was discussed the first day, then repeated every day thereafter."

Horst Schulze CONT

"I reminded them several times the first day, "You are special. But we didn't select you to work for us; we want you to share our dream to be the best in the world."

We identified the 20 things that would make us a better company and we repeated one thing every day. For example, number 11: if you get a complaint, you own it, you apologize, you listen, you show empathy. In 20 days, that would be repeated. We read letters to our staff from guests complimenting us on that. At every hotel, in every department, before every shift, we shared that feedback. Whether you were in Shanghai or Berlin or Philadelphia, it was the same. This created the same culture."

various forms of telehealth and greater connectivity with patients after the delivery of care. This will likely precipitate a phenomenon that caught the hospitality industry by surprise: the popularity of self-service.

Having prided themselves on the delivery of great guest service, traditional hoteliers were shocked to discover many guests were happy to serve themselves rather than suffer through the wait times that often characterized the delivery of traditional hotel services. They willingly made their own reservations, checked themselves in upon arrival, poured their own coffee in the morning, microwaved a snack in their room, even checked themselves out remotely when ready to depart.

Similar trends emerged in the restaurant and airline industries. Now, there are clearly many elements of healthcare service delivery that require staff intervention because of their nature. Yet, there are also many that would lend themselves to self-service if such an option were offered.

SOLICITATION OF FEEDBACK

The rapid adoption of increasingly user-friendly mobile technology will also make it much easier for healthcare service providers to address an important deficiency revealed in our Gap Survey: the failure of many to solicit and use feedback from patients on their experiences. This will yield actionable insights on service problems both during and after the delivery of healthcare services, even in real-time, thereby enabling providers to rectify problems as they occur. These insights may also be used to determine which services could be offered with a performance guarantee.

PERSONALIZED MEDICINE

Perhaps the greatest impact consumers' growing use of technology will have on the delivery of healthcare is the degree to which providers will be able to capture patient data and use it to build profiles that reflect individual habits and preferences. The term personalized medicine will no longer be reserved for use by clinicians. Rather, it will also apply to the way patients are served. This development will facilitate healthcare service providers' ability to introduce patient recognition and reward programs that build loyal patronage over time.

TRANSPARENCY AND COMPETITION

The march toward greater transparency in the pricing of healthcare services is inevitable, borne of the confluence of increased competition for patients and the ease with which consumers will be able to access this information. Deloitte Research provides an interesting assessment of the potential impact this may have on the contour of future demand: 60% of patients stated they were more likely to choose a provider that compared its prices to the local healthcare market.[6] The objections of payors and providers notwithstanding, market disintermediation will accelerate the impact of this trend, just as it did in the hospitality and transportation industries. Consumer sentiment on this controversial topic is clear:

- Seven out of 10 respondents in our Gap Survey agreed on, "The importance of knowing how much I have to pay for the (healthcare) service before I receive it," (top three boxes on a 10-point scale), yet just slightly more than half (53%) acknowledged they knew how much they would have to pay.

- The Trump administration's 2019 executive order directing hospitals to publish select service prices notwithstanding, both compliance and enforcement have been lagging, presumably a reflection of the reticence of providers to disclose this information. We believe growing consumer demand for greater transparency will accelerate compliance in the months ahead.

- The Transparency of Coverage rule published by the US CMS requires payors to publish the cost of most healthcare services they have negotiated with providers effective July 1, 2022. This will occur over the protestations of payors.

DISTINCTIONS BETWEEN SERVICE AND TREATMENT

The acceleration of healthcare pricing transparency will herald the arrival of the potentially controversial service strategy we mentioned earlier in this book: the premise that all patients are not created equal when it comes to the way they are served. Again, to clarify, the distinction we make is how they are served, not treated. Healthcare service providers segment and track patients by insurance and/or payment type today. Yet, we believe this segmentation will mature to include groups of "like" patients defined by additional considerations such as the price they are prepared to pay, when they want to be treated, the amenities they seek, the frequency of their visitation and, ultimately, their loyalty to the same service provider or healthcare system over time. One wonders whether actual clinical outcomes will also become a basis of product differentiation, with providers who deliver superior outcomes charging and receiving more. This type of pricing is already evident in the contract rates payors negotiate for clinical services with preeminent hospitals and other care providers, yet patients have no visibility into these proprietary arrangements. Perhaps they will as the march toward pricing transparency continues.

TRANSFORMED SERVICESCAPE

The servicescape created and maintained by healthcare service providers will also undergo significant transformation in the years ahead as providers focus more on atmospherics and the environmental aspects of patient engagement. These improvements will reduce patients' anxiety and help them understand the quality of service they receive by making it more tangible. The components of the RATER system will become more important to healthcare service providers for the following reasons:

- With information everywhere, consumers will continue to believe they are qualified to make more informed healthcare decisions. Yet, they will continue to look for cues to validate their healthcare decisions. These cues will extend well beyond the sense of hospitality provided by healthcare service staff to include all aspects of the servicescape, such as the color, comfort, and configuration of waiting rooms, the ease of wayfinding, and the like. Competition for self-insured patients or patients with attractive commercial health insurance will therefore intensify. These patients will be required to offset the low rates of provider reimbursement paid by the Centers for Medicare and Medicaid. As this competition increases, healthcare service providers will seek more ways to differentiate themselves to attract these patients. One way will be through manipulating the different elements of the servicescape. As an example, academic researchers are beginning to investigate the influence of the servicescape on patients' mental health.[7] Astute healthcare service providers will redesign their facilities consistent with the findings of this research to attract more patients away from competitors.

- Consumers' growing interest in, and embrace of, living more healthy lifestyles will also require healthcare service providers to lend greater emphasis to preventative programs while continuing to ensure clinical excellence. This is especially true for Millennial and GenZ patients who, arguably, have taken far greater interest in their wellness than their parents. This is evidenced by their embrace of the benefits of exercise and improved nutrition, insistence on better work/life balance, and greater appreciation for the benefits of a lifestyle that enhances well-being, not one defined primarily by the acquisition of material possessions. Any programs developed must be consumable and made available on demand through popular media. However, they must also include opportunities for participants of similar backgrounds to engage on social media. Such an evolution will require hospitals and healthcare systems to reposition themselves as centers of community wellness, not just destinations for acute or specialty care.

RECOGNITION AND REWARD PROGRAMS

Healthcare service providers will acknowledge the importance of recognition and reward programs as a strategy to build patient loyalty and cultivate lifetime value. Service providers use loyalty programs to encourage their customers to identify themselves as they make repeat purchases. This self-identification allows providers to collect and track customers' purchase data and discover their preferences. The information may then be merged with other data sources to provide detailed profiles of customers' preferences.

Hospitality service providers use these data to make their brands more attractive to hotel/restaurant owners who may be interested in affiliating through some form or licensing or ownership, a process called *flagging*. These owners seek brands that can help them "put heads in beds." The data captured in loyalty programs can show potential owners a brand's potential to facilitate this. In turn, the addition of new locations accelerates growth of the brand's loyalty database, thereby strengthening the brand.

The introduction of loyalty programs to the healthcare industry will catalyze a similar phenomenon. It will enable healthcare networks and systems to expand their systems through licensing, drive incremental revenue, spread fixed costs across multiple facilities, increase purchasing power for required goods and services, distribute marketing expenses across multiple facilities, and provide patients with more convenient options to access care.

CONSOLIDATION

Mergers and acquisitions among healthcare service providers will continue apace. The consolidation that has occurred in recent years—hospital systems, physician practices, even healthcare service suppliers—will accelerate as healthcare service providers seek to grow their geographic footprint, expand addressable markets, amortize operating expenses, and serve more new patients. In turn, this trend will lead providers to introduce patient recognition and reward programs that encourage repeat patronage within these expanding networks, build loyalty, and capture a greater share of their lifetime value – just as they have in the hospitality industry.

EMBRACING HAPPINESS

Healthcare service providers will embrace the hospitality industry philosophy that "happy employees mean happy customers" for the simple reason that happy employees are more likely to create positive moments of truth with customers than unhappy ones. The superior ratings given to hospitality service providers on the following measures of customer engagement in our Gap Survey underscore the importance of this:

Michael Leven, former President and CEO of Holiday Inn Hotels & Resorts, and one of the most successful franchisors of lodging brands, believes franchising is a strategy that could accelerate the growth of healthcare systems if executed properly:

"Prominent healthcare brands could accelerate their growth through smart franchising if they maintained a consistent quality of care. But this growth strategy probably makes the most sense for operators of limited-service or specialized clinics rather than acute care hospitals because of the challenges associated with delivering consistent quality when providing more comprehensive healthcare."

- The people I interact with are eager to serve me.

- The people I interact with make me feel welcome.

- It's easy to resolve disputes I have about the value of the service I received.

- The provider resolves any problems I express about my experience quickly.

- The provider tries to make me feel satisfied with the service I received.

In chapter one, we introduced the Gap Model of Service Quality, which included five reasons for potential service gaps that could influence customer sentiment about the quality of service received and corresponding levels of satisfaction. Reason number three pertained to the inability of the organization to hire the right staff to deliver the service. This is often the result of poor human resource policies.

An article in the *Cornell Hospitality Quarterly*[8] revealed that the strategic levers human resource departments use to retain the best employees may also be used to create happy employees. These include: (1) how employees are recruited, selected, and trained; (2) how employees are on onboarded and mentored; (3) how management communicates with employees; and (4), how employees are recognized and rewarded. These strategic levers also help define the overall culture of the organization. This is another critical factor that leads to more meaningful employee engagement.

Healthcare service providers should also ask themselves the following questions. The answers will also reveal ways to create happy employees:

- Are you the preferred employer?

- Are you hiring for service competencies and service inclination?

- Are you competing for the best people?

- Are you measuring and rewarding strong service performers?

- Are you treating employees as customers?

- Are you including employees in the company's vision?

- Are you developing service-oriented internal processes?

- Are you providing supportive technology and equipment?

- Are you measuring internal service quality?

- Are you promoting teamwork?

- Are you empowering employees?

- Are you training for technical and interactive skills?

A DISCIPLINED COMMITMENT TO IMPACT ANALYSIS

Finally, assessing the impact of investments intended to enhance the patient experience will require a disciplined commitment to the analysis of the impact of the services rendered. Performance over time should be evaluated with respect to five categories of measurement:

1. Sentiment expressed about the provider in patient-authored communications.

2. The provider's reputation among key constituents, both offline and online, including existing patients, prospective patients, the public, the clinical community, and payors.

3. The incidence and trending of patient satisfaction and repeat patronage.

4. The incidence and trending of patient loyalty.

Dr. Jason Wolf, President & CEO of The Beryl Institute.

"The integrated experience patients have in healthcare, beyond just the clinical outcome, is a fundamental determinant of their assessment of the quality of care they receive. For that reason, healthcare organizations must also have an unwavering focus on caring for their employees as well. You cannot provide a positive experience for those you serve unless you also ensure one for those who show up every day to serve them.

People ask three things of their healthcare providers, in addition to a positive clinical outcome:

(1) listen to me,

(2) communicate clearly in a way I can understand, and

(3) treat me with dignity and respect."

Maurie Markman, MD, suggests healthcare providers look at hospitality-based loyalty programs as a model.

"In the hospitality sector, quality experiences are incentives for customers to become loyal. In healthcare, loyalty should be based on positive outcomes, because satisfaction will keep bringing patients and their families back to the system.

As for the role of hospitality in healthcare? It should be to link payment with outcomes and patient satisfaction, just like in the hospitality industry. But no provider has ever done this. I think it should be done though, through pilot projects that are watched very carefully, all measured in the same way."

5. Financial results.

The insights that derive from these metrics should serve as complementary lenses through which to assess the overall quality of the patient experience and corresponding financial results.

The relative importance of each category of measurement will presumably vary by both the mission and culture of the host enterprise. For example, the weight assigned to financial return may be greater for a for-profit than not-for-profit enterprise.

Reputational assessments may be of greater importance to organizations seeking to achieve and/or retain special certifications or solicit top talent to join their enterprise. Faith-based providers might ascribe higher value to the profile of patients served. Ultimately, however, the final algorithm should reflect the values embraced by the enterprise.

Summary

We began this journey by deconstructing Roger Conway's experience getting a colonoscopy, followed by his weekend in Las Vegas. Now, you might dismiss such a comparison as apocryphal because of the fundamentally different motivation for each, but there were many common moments of truth: booking the appointment or reservation, pre-arrival preparations, the ambiance of the servicescape, knowing the price of the service before it was delivered, arrival of an unexpected bill, the presence or absence of some type of recognition to build loyalty, and a request for feedback on the entire experience. We now know these expressions of hospitality have a significant and enduring impact on the patient experience, oftentimes more so than the clinical outcome.

We also know much of the cost of implementing hospitality principles is already embedded in the profit and loss of healthcare service providers. Absent is a fresh approach to composing enterprise mission/vision/values in a way that acknowledges the anxieties, frustrations, and hopes of patients. And recognition that all patients do not have to be served equally, so long as they are treated equally.

Our PAEER model synthesizes the five components necessary to enhance the patient experience by introducing hospitality principles. We encourage healthcare service providers, large or small, public or private, for-profit or not-for-profit, to acknowledge that many of these principles are worthy of adoption.

As stated at the outset, some will be easy to implement. Others more difficult, even controversial. Many challenge conventional wisdom about how healthcare should be delivered. But we are confident providers who may now be inspired to embrace these principles will enhance the patient experience they provide. We are equally confident the increasingly loyal patients they serve will acknowledge and applaud the more hospitable healthcare they receive.

Dr. Leonard Berry offers additional advice for healthcare service providers, and a provocative insight into the mindset of patients that obstructs open, honest dialogue with clinicians:

"Healthcare service providers should ask 'What matters to you?' not just 'What is the matter with you?'

Patients often act like hostages in the presence of their physicians, borne of a reluctance to challenge clinicians' observations or recommendations. This 'hostage bargaining syndrome' is evident in clinical research and derives from patients' lack of confidence in their ability to interpret much of what is communicated by their physicians. Clinicians should be mindful of this unexpressed sentiment when they engage with patients."

Contributors

WE WOULD LIKE TO EXPRESS our deep appreciation for the valuable contribution made to the insights and observations presented in this book by the clinicians, administrators, educators, entrepreneurs, and investors who graciously agreed to share their expertise:

Jeff Arnold, Co-founder, Chairman and Chief Executive Officer of Sharecare

Dr. Leonard Berry, Distinguished University Professor, Texas A&M University

Mostafa Boutajrit, Vice President of Loyalty, Financial Services and Customer Assurance, Caesars Entertainment

Shruti Buckley, Senior Vice President and Global Brand Head, Hampton by Hilton

Adam Burke, Former Senior Vice President, HHonors, Hilton Corporation

Dr. Greg Burke, Chief Experience Officer, Geisinger Health System

Marci Carson, Editor

Antoine Chahwan, President of Hotel Operations – Americas East, Four Seasons Hotels & Resorts

Dr. Fred DeMicco, Professor and Director, School of Hotel & Restaurant Management, Northern Arizona University

Emma Elzinga, Graphic Designer, Indigo River Publishing

Rick Evans, Senior Vice President and Chief Experience Officer, New York Presbyterian Hospital

Deborah Froese, Executive Editor, Indigo River Publishing

Craig Granger, Graphics Designer

Laurence Geller, Chairman, Geller Capital Partners

Toni Land, Head of Clinical Healthcare Experience, Medallia, Inc.

Michael Leven, Former President & Chief Executive Officer, Holiday Inn Hotels & Resorts

Winston Lord, Former Chief Evangelist, OpenTable

Edward Mady, Former West Coast Regional Director, Dorchester Collection

Josh Margolis, Vice President of Customer Journey, Caesars Entertainment

Dr. Maurie Markman, President of Medicine & Science, Cancer Treatment Centers of America Global, Inc.

Dr. James Merlino, Chief Clinical Transformation Officer, Cleveland Clinic

Laurence Minsky, Associate Professor of Communication, Columbia College

Mirjana Munetic, Associate Principal, ZGF Architects

David Norton, Chairman, GALE Partners

Horst Schulze, Former President & Chief Executive Officer, Ritz-Carlton Hotel Company

Dr. Mardelle Shepley, Professor and Director, Cornell University Institute for Healthy Futures

Gerard van Grinsven, Former President & Chief Executive Officer, Cancer Treatment Centers of America Global, Inc.

Tripp Welch, Vice Chair of Quality Management Services, Mayo Clinic

Charles White, Principal, Skyline Art

Dr. Jason Wolf, Chief Executive Officer, The Beryl Institute

Dr. Cristobal Young, Associate Professor of Sociology, Cornell University

With our sincere gratitude,
Stowe Shoemaker, PhD, and Peter Yesawich, PhD.

Acknowledgments

THIS BOOK COULD NOT HAVE been written without the incredible insights I have learned from those I connected with in hospitality, healthcare, and academia. It also could not have been written with the help of others.

Frank and Jane Emanual introduced me to the world of hospitality when I was an undergraduate in college. I continue to marvel at how they understood—before many others—the relationship between employee satisfaction, guest satisfaction and what it means to be hospitable. They are true hoteliers. Andrew and Peggy Cherng, the founders of the Panda Restaurant Group, of which Panda Express is a part, showed me that with proper systems and a laser focus on employee and customer satisfaction, it is possible to be hospitable across a multi-chain restaurant company with thousands of employees.

Sharon Messimer first introduced me to the possibility of the intersection between hospitality and healthcare when she was working with Memorial Hermann Healthcare System in Houston, Texas. Dr. Marshall Hicks and Dr. Joey Steele enabled me to continue to investigate this intersection—and make meaningful change—by providing me with a joint appointment at University of Texas, MD Anderson Cancer Center. Of all the projects I have undertaken over the years, I am most proud of my work with MD Anderson Cancer Center. Ms. Messimer, Dr. Hicks, and Dr. Steele were visionaries and continue to be so today.

Dr. Robert Lewis and Dr. Mark Renaghan, my two academic mentors, taught me how to look beyond the surface and use rigorous thinking and analysis to truly understand a given phenomenon. I hope I have made them proud.

Erin Nicole Trasmano, an architecture undergraduate at UNLV, spent much time helping me gather all the necessary permissions and ensure all formatting of references were correct. She is extremely talented and has an amazing career ahead of her. Craig Granger deserves a huge "thank you" for all the wonderful graphics in the book. Angela Ramsey, a colleague at UNLV, deserves credit for helping me be a better writer. Ashley Trevitz was instrumental in keeping the project on schedule as we began to write this book. Ashley is an amazing young woman and my wife and I are honored to have her part of our family. An author could not ask for better support and friendship than that provided by Erin, Craig, Angela, and Ashley. My heartfelt thanks to all of you.

And no acknowledgment would be complete without thanks for the one person who has truly guided me throughout all my journeys and provided specific comments that guided the direction of this book and found through our research at MD Anderson Cancer Center that patients wanted to be treated like loved family members. This is my best friend and my wife, Dr. Martha Shoemaker. I have been blessed for such a loving and supportive lifelong partner.

– *Stowe Shoemaker, PhD*

∾

Everyone has a story about a personal healthcare experience gone wrong. But stories about healthcare experiences gone right are what inspired this book and our exploration of how healthcare service providers could ensure more of them through the adoption of principles of hospitality.

I am privileged to have witnessed the incredibly positive effect hospitality can have on the patient experience among individuals fighting the most feared diagnosis: cancer. For this I am deeply grateful to the Chairman of Cancer Treatment Centers of America® (CTCA), Richard J Stephenson, an indefatigable and uncompromising advocate of delivering exceptional patient-centered care who enlisted my support in the pursuit of his mission for 10 years of my career; to his empathetic physician son, Dr. Christopher Stephenson, who graciously invited me to shadow him on patient rounds which oftentimes included difficult "destiny" conversations; and to Dr. Maurie Markman, President of Medicine & Science at CTCA, a renowned oncologist who helped me understand both the power and limitations of his expertise while providing an immensely helpful critique of the applicability of my ideas in practice.

Most of all, I want to express my heartfelt thanks to the patients of CTCA whom I was privileged to meet, know, and serve. Through them that I came to understand the remarkable motivational and therapeutic benefits of hospitality applied to healthcare.

Special recognition is also due Ashley Trevitz, Barbara Lewis and Marta Soligo for their assistance organizing content, scheduling and hosting the interviews we conducted with numerous contributors, excerpts of which appear throughout the book; Craig Granger for his patience and guidance designing the numerous graphics; Emma Elzinga for her creative composition of the book; and Deborah Froese and Marci Carson for their invaluable counsel guiding our articulation of the contents.

And no acknowledgement would be complete without thanks for the one person who endured the many hours I spent drafting, discarding, and rewriting multiple versions of the manuscript that eventually became this book: my wife, Paris.

– Peter C. Yesawich, PhD

Endnotes

CHAPTER 1

1   "Unparalleled Customer Intelligence," Benchmarks, American Customer Satisfaction Index, accessed August 10, 2022, https://www.theacsi.org/our-industries/.

2   "National per capita health expenditures in the Unites States," Statista, 2020.

3   J.O. Hero et al., "Understanding What Makes Americans Less Satisfied With Their Healthcare System: An International Comparison," Health Affairs, March 2016.

4   Anna Wilde Mathews, "A Family's Health Insurance Cost More Than $22,000 in 2021, Survey Finds," *Wall Street Journal, November 10, 2021.*

5   "The Holiday Inn story," Kemmons Wilson Companies, accessed February 2, 2023, http://kwilson.com/our-story/holiday-inn/.

6   Bionic Disco, "Holiday Inn 'Surprise!' Commercial, 1975" YouTube, September 5, 2021, https://www.youtube.com/watch?v=WNh5uY1ePcA.

7   J. Wirtz, C. Lovelock, *Services Marketing: 8th Edition (Singapore: World Scientific Publishing CO Pte Ltd., 2016).*

8   "4 Main Components of a Service (Explained With a Diagram)," Your Article Library, accessed March 8, 2023, https://www.yourarticlelibrary.com/services/4-main-components-of-a-service-explained-with-diagram/34016.

9   V. Zeithaml, M. J. Bitner, *Services Marketing, (New York: McGraw-Hill, 1996), 518.*

10   S. Shoemaker, R. Lewis, "Customer Loyalty in Hotels," International Journal of Hospitality Management 18, no. 4 (1990): 345–370.

CHAPTER 2

1   Irit Hochberg et al., "Assessment of the Frequency of Online Searches for Symptoms Before Diagnosis: Analysis of Archival Data," *Journal of Internet Medical Research, June 3, 2020.*

2   John Anderer, "Two in Five Have Misdiagnosed Themselves With Serious Disease After Googling Symptoms," Let's Get Checked, November 18, 2019, https://studyfinds.org/two-in-five-have-misdiagnosed-themselves-with-serious-disease-after-googling-symptoms/.

3   Laura Sydell, "Fake Patient Reviews are Making it Increasingly Hard to Seek Medical Help on Google, Yelp and Other Directory Sites," *The Washington Post, June 5, 2021.*

4   "Portrait of American Travelers," MMGY Global, 2021.

5   "Online Reviews Study: Restaurants and Reviews," GatherUp, November 5, 2018.

6   C. Robert, S. Shoemaker, "Value Pricing: Another View and a Research Example," Cornell Hotel and Restaurant Administration Quarterly 38, no. 2, (April 1997): 44-54.

7   "Trump Administration Announces Historic Price Transparency Requirements to Promote Competition and Lower Healthcare Costs for all Americans," Centers for Medicare and Medicaid Services, November 15, 2019.

8   "The Staggering Cost of Health Insurance Sludge," Insights by Stanford Business, February 23, 2021.

9   Joseph Tarnowski, "'Guest' vs. 'Customer': Does it really matter?"

LinkedIn, March 29, 2015, https://www.linkedin.com/pulse/
guest-vs-customer-does-really-matter-joseph-tarnowski/.

10   "Difference Between a Guest and a Customer,"
     Hospitality Career Tips for Students, Savvy Hotelier,
     July 27, 2019, https://www.savvyhotelier.net/post/
     difference-between-a-guest-and-a-customer.

11   Julia Faria, "U.S. Healthcare Local Ad Spend 2017-2021, By
     Format," Statista, January 6, 2023.

12   "AHA Data and Insights," American Hospital Association, April
     2020, https://www.ahadata.com/topics/hospital-data.

13   U.S. Travel Association, "U.S. Travel Answer Sheet," May 20,
     2022, https://www.ustravel.org/research/us-travel-answer-sheet.

14   Flori Needle, "10 Consumer Behavior Models (& Which One
     Applies to Your Business)," HubSpot, December 10, 2021,
     https://blog.hubspot.com/service/consumer-behavior-model.

15   Stowe Shoemaker, R.C. Lewis, and P. C. Yesawich, "Marketing
     Leadership in Hospitality and Tourism: Strategies and Tactics
     for a Competitive Advantage," (Upper Saddle River, NJ:
     Prentice Hall, 2006), 174.

16   Bryan Wroten, "Hampton's Evolution From Economy
     to an Industry Leader," CoStar, June 14, 2018,
     https://www.costar.com/article/1543382795/
     hamptons-evolution-from-economy-to-an-industry-leader.

17   Ronald A and Paulus, "ProvenCare: Geisinger's Model for Care
     Transformation Through Innovative Clinical Initiatives and
     Value Creation," American Health & Drug Benefits, accessed
     June 21, 2022, https://pubmed.ncbi.nlm.nih.gov/25126281/.

CHAPTER 3

1   Joseph Rodgers Steele, MD, Kyle Jones, PhD, Ryan K. Clarke,
    MHA, Stowe Shoemaker, PhD, "Health Care Delivery Meets

Hospitality: A Pilot Study in Radiology," *Journal of the American College of Radiology 12, no. 6 (June 2015).*

2   Vilert A. Loving, MD, Richard L. Ellis, MD, Robert Rippee, MBA, Joseph R. Steele, MD, Donald F. Schomer, MD, Stowe Shoemaker, PhD, "Time Time is Not on Our Side: How Radiology Practices Should Manage Customer Queues," *Journal of the American College of Radiology 14 (2017): 1481-1488.*

3   Interestingly, patients claimed 45 minutes was about the time they expected to wait. Without this information, management would have tried to get the wait time to zero at great expense. The 45-minute window gave them time provide better experience and more time to implement components of the RATER system.

4   "Types of Restaurants: 10 Common Restaurant Categories," MasterClass, June 7, 2021, https://www.masterclass.com/articles/types-of-restaurants-explained.

5   "What Hoteliers Need to Know About Data Privacy Protection," Trivago Business Blog, February 7, 2019, https://businessblog.trivago.com/data-privacy-protection-hotel-businesses/.

6   "Health Insurance Portability and Accountability Act of 1996 (HIPPA)," https://www.cdc.gov/phlp/publications/topic/hipaa.html.

7   "Portrait of American Travelers," MMGY Global, 2021.

CHAPTER 4

1   "Iatrophobia (Fear of Doctors)," Cleveland Clinic, December 10, 2021, https://my.clevelandclinic.org/health/diseases/22191-iatrophobia-fear-of-doctors.

2   Melissa Welby, "The Anxious Patient: How to Calm a Patient Down to Improve Care," Wolters Kluwer, March 17, 2020, https://www.wolterskluwer.com/en/expert-insights/the-anxious-patient-how-to-calm-a-patient-down-to-improve-care.

3   Image received by Stowe Shoemaker through personal correspon-
    dence with The Inn at The Market upon booking a reservation
    in July 202. Used with with permission.

4   "Grubhub launches 'Grubhub Guarantee' to Promise On-Time
    Delivery and Lowest Prices," *OSR Industry News, July 12,
    2021.*

5   Ronald A and Paulus, "ProvenCare: Geisinger's Model for
    Care Transformation through Innovative Clinical Initiatives
    and Value Creation," interview, American Health & Drug
    Benefits, accessed June 21, 2022, https://pubmed.ncbi.nlm.nih.
    gov/25126281/.

6   "The Intersection Between Value and Telehealth," Center for
    Connected Medicine, September 2021.

7   Juliet Deltalima, "Servicesscape," January 2, 2023. https://en.wiki-
    pedia.org/wiki/Servicescape.

8   Daire Hooper et al., "The Servicescape as an Antecedent to
    Service Quality and Behavioral Intentions," Journal of Services
    Marketing 27, no. 4 (2013): 271–280, http://eprints.maynoo-
    thuniversity.ie/6594/1/JC-Servicescape-Antecedent.pdf.

9   Cristobal Young and Xinxiang Chen, "Patients as Consumers in
    the Market for Medicine: The Halo Effect of Hospitality," Social
    Forces 99, no. 2 (December 2020): 504-531.

10 "What is a Simple Definition of the Physical
    Environment?" Enotes, accessed August 15,
    2022, https://www.enotes.com/homework-help/
    what-simple-deffinition-physical-environment-thank-369776.

11 "Ian Schrager," Wikimedia Foundation, modified June 16, 2022,
    08:43, https://en.wikipedia.org/wiki/Ian_Schrager.

12 "What Should an Architect Keep in Mind When Designing a
    Hotel?" The Hotelier Academy, 2019.

13 "Hotel Interior Design, Part 1: The Psychology of Color and
    2018 Trends," Fohlio, 2018.

14   "The Psychology of Colors in the Hospitality Business," Simextra: The Outdoor Furniture Specialists, accessed March 3, 2023, https://www.simexa.com/the-psychology-of-colors-in-hospitality-business-wholesale-outdoor-furniture/.

15   "Six Ways Light Can Affect Your Emotions," Mental Floss, October 30, 2016, https://www.mentalfloss.com/article/88046/6-ways-light-can-affect-your-emotions.

16   Mohamed Boubekri et al., "Impact of Windows and Daylight Exposure on Overall Health and Sleep Quality of Office Workers: A Case-Control Pilot Study," National Library of Medicine, June 15, 2014, https://pubmed.ncbi.nlm.nih.gov/24932139/.

17   "Transforming Indoor Spaces," StayWell Rooms, accessed June 20, 2022, https://staywellrooms.com/about/.

18   Marta Zaraska, "The Sense of Smell in Humans is More Powerful Than We Think," Discover, October 10, 2017, https://www.discovermagazine.com/mind/the-sense-of-smell-in-humans-is-more-powerful-than-we-think.

19   "Inside the Invisible But Influential World of Scent Branding," Harvard Business Review, April 11, 2018.

20   D.V. Zemke, S. Shoemaker, "A Sociable Atmosphere: Ambient Scent's Effect on Social Interaction," Cornell Hotel and Restaurant Administration Quarterly 49, no. 3 (2008): 317-329.

21   Laura Fredericks, "Why do Hotels Smell so Good? Complete Hotel Scent Guide," Cvent Blog, June 16, 2021, https://www.cvent.com/en/blog/hospitality/why-do-hotels-smell-so-good.

22   Scott McCartney, "Why does the Holiday Inn smell like musk?" The Wall Street Journal, November 8, 2017, https://www.wsj.com/articles/why-does-the-holiday-inn-smell-like-musk-1510160764.

23   "The Good Time Hotel has a new signature scent," *BAZAAR, March 8, 2022.*

24 "Ambient Scenting and Odor Control Systems for Hospitals," Air-Scent International, January 23, 2020, https://www.airscent. com/hospital-ambient-scenting-odor-control.

25 "Music: Every Scene Has a Soundtrack," last accessed March 6, 2023, https://w-hotels.marriott.com/about/music.

26 "Starbucks Music," last accessed March 6, 2023, https://www. starbucks.com/rewards/music.

27 "How Kimpton's Lauren Bucherie Creates Soundtracks That are Music to Guests' Ears," Hotel Management, August 13, 2018.

28 "In Store, Atmosphere Counts. And Shoppers Say Music Helps," Marketing Charts, June 27, 2017.

29 "Indoor Hospital Wayfinding and Navigation," *Pointr, 2022.*

30 The unbreakable rules of successful wayfinding design," Encompass, January 30, 2017, http://www.encompasssign.com/ blog/the-unbreakable-rules-of-successful-wayfinding-design.

CHAPTER 5

1 "Elevating the Human Experience in Healthcare," The Beryl Institute, June 20, 2022, http://www.theberylinstitute.org.

2 Jan Carlson, Moments of Truth (Cambridge, Mass.: Ballinger Publishing Company, 1989).

3 Shep Hyken, "The New Moment of Truth in Business," Forbes, April 9, 2016, https://www.forbes.com/sites/shephyken/2016/04/09/ new-moment-of-truth-in-business/?sh=55d7297a38d9.

4 "Marketing Campaigns in the Banking Sector have Average Response Rates of 2%-5%," Eventricity, last accessed March 6, 2023, https://www.eventricity.biz.

5 "The Beverly Hills Hotel," Trip Advisor, December 5, 2021, https://www.tripadvisor.com/Hotel_Review-g32070-d76093- Reviews-The_Beverly_Hills_Hotel-Beverly_Hills_California. html.

6   Elizabeth Rhodes, Andrea Romano, "25 Best Theme Parks in the United States," Travel & Leisure, April 26, 2021, https://www.travelandleisure.com/attractions/amusement-parks/tripadvisor-best-theme-parks-in-america.

7   Bob Adams, "7 Guest Service Guidelines: Old School Disney at Its Best," 27Gen, December 15, 2014, https://27gen.com/2014/12/15/7-guest-service-guidelines-old-school-disney-at-its-best/.

8   Michaela Barnes, "Hampton by Hilton's New 100% Guarantee," Hospitalitynet, January 19, 2017, https://www.hospitalitynet.org/news/4080485.html.

9   "Gold Standards," The Ritz-Carlton, accessed June 21, 2022, https://www.ritzcarlton.com/en/about/gold-standards.

10   "The Malcolm Baldrige National Quality Award," The Ritz-Carlton, accessed June 21, 2021, http://news.ritzcarlton.com/the-malcolm-baldrige-national-quality-award/.

11   YouGov Best Brand Rankings in the United States, white paper, 2020.

12   "HCAHPS: Patients Perspectives of Care," Centers for Medicare & Medicaid Services.

13   "Office of Patient Experience," Cleveland Clinic, accessed June 21, 2022, https://my.clevelandclinic.org/departments/patient-experience/depts/office-patient-experience.

14   Joseph Rodgers Steele, MD, Kyle Jones, PhD, Ryan K. Clarke, MHA, Stowe Shoemaker, PhD, "Health Care Delivery Meets Hospitality: A Pilot Study in Radiology," Journal of the American College of Radiology 12, no. 6 (June 2015).

15   "Waystar Survey Finds Patients are More Stressed About Medical Bills Than About Care," Waystar, November 2020.

16   Dario Melpignano, "10 Inspirational Customer Experience Quotes," LinkedIn, February 12, 2015, https://www.linkedin.

com/pulse/10-inspirational-customer-experience-quotes-im-prove-dario-melpignano/.

CHAPTER 6

1 "The Patient Perspective, 2019: Online Online Reputation Survey," PatientPop, 2019.

2 "How Patients Feel About Emerging Healthcare Technology," Software Advice, March 2020.

3 "RepuGen Patient Review Survey, 2021," RepuGen, ac-cessed March 8, 2023, https://www.repugen.com/patient-review-survey-2021.

4 "HCAHPS: Patients' Perspectives of Care Survey," Centers for Medicare & Medicaid Services, accessed on March 6, 2023, https://www.cms.gov/Medicare/Quality-Initiatives-Patient-Assessment-Instruments/HospitalQualityInits/HospitalHCAHPS.

5 "Early Warning Signals: How Experience Signals Can Drive Your Business Forward," Medallia, accessed March 7, 2023, https://www.medallia.com/resource/early-warning-signals/.

6 "What is Customer Experience Management?" Qualtrics, accessed June 21, 2022, https://www.qualtrics.com/experience-management/customer/customer-experience-management-platform/.

7 "Global Trust In Advertising," Nielsen, September 2015, https://www.nielsen.com/insights/2015/global-trust-in-advertising-2015/.

8 "The History of Net Promoter," Net Promoter System, accessed June 21, 2022, https://www.netpromotersystem.com/about/history-of-net-promoter/.

9 Roger Hallowell, Abby Hansen, "A Taste of Frankenmuth: A Town in Michigan Thinks About Word-of-Mouth Referral," Harvard

Business School Publishing, 1999, Product Number 9-800-029.

CHAPTER 7

1 "How to Take an Analytical Approach to New Patient Retention," Mercury Healthcare, 2021.

2 Max Starkov, "Are Hotel Loyalty and Rewards Programs Enough to Keep Customers Loyal to the Brand?" HospitalityNet, October 2021, https://www.hospitalitynet.org/opin-ion/4106862.html.

3 "Top 100 Most Valuable Airline Loyalty Programs," OnPoint, 2020.

4 "41 Customer Loyalty Statistics and 10 Benefits for SMEs," P2P Marketing, 2022.

5 "Key Brand Loyalty Statistics," Yotpo, 2019.

6 "Loyalty in Healthcare," PK Global, November, 2021.

7 John Bowen, Stowe Shoemaker, "The Antecedents and Consequences of Customer Loyalty," February, *Cornell Hotel and Restaurant Administration Quarterly 39, no. 1 (February 1998): 12-25.*

8 John Deighton, Stowe Shoemaker, "Hilton HHonors Worldwide: Loyalty Wars," Harvard Business School Publishing, revised November 2005.

9 Deanna Ting, "What Private Equity Giant Blackstone has meant to Hilton," Skift, May 18, 2018, https://skift.com/2018/05/18/what-private-equity-giant-blackstone-has-meant-to-hilton/.

10 "Honors ins Big at 2020 Points Guy Awards, sweeping all hotel categories," Points Guy, December 2020.

CHAPTER 9

1 "Cancer Network Partners," MD Anderson Center, accessed June 21, 2022, https://www.mdanderson.org/about-md-anderson/

our-locations/md-anderson-cancer-network/network-partners. html.

2   "City of Hope to Acquire Cancer Treatment Centers of America," City of Hope, December 2021.

3   Sarah Thomas, "Physician networks—one piece of the puzzle for improving performance," Deloitte, February 19, 2019, https://www2.deloitte.com/us/en/blog/health-care-blog/2019/ health-care-current-february19-2019.html.

4   Omer Minkara, "Customer Operations in Healthcare: Building Blocks to Transform Patient Experiences and Minimize Operational Complexity," Aberdeen Research, June 2021, https://www.servicenow.com/lpayr/aberdeen-customer-opera- tions-in-healthcare.html.

5   "The Role Online Reviews Play in Patients Choosing a Physician," Vizium360, 2021.

6   "Putting a Price on Transparency," Deloitte Insights, 2020.

7   "Designing Servicescapes for Transformative Service Conversations: Lessons from Mental Health Services," Gopaldas, Siebert, Ertimur, Journal of Consumer Marketing, 2021.

8   "So What Makes it so Great: An Analysis of Human Resources Practices Among Fortune's Best Companies to Work For," Cornell Hospitality Quarterly, Hinkin and Tracey, 2010.

Service Variables Rated and Significance Testing

RESPONDENTS WERE ASKED TO RATE the extent to which 24 different service variables common to both the hospitality and healthcare industries reflected their experience with each of the five service provider categories. Tests of statistical significance were conducted on the differences observed in the related percentages. The results are summarized in Figure 1.

Respondents were also asked to rate the extent to which the following statements reflected their sentiments toward each of the five service provider categories on the stated topics. Tests of statistical significance were conducted on the differences observed in the related percentages. The results are summarized in Figure 2.

SERVICE VARIABLE COLUMN REFERENCE FOR TEST OF STATISTICAL SIGNIFICANCE AT 95% CONFIDENCE	STAYING IN HOTEL/MOTEL/RESORT* A	DINING OUT FOR LUNCH/DINNER* B	VISITING A HOSPITAL* C	VISITING A WALK-IN CLINIC* D	VISITING A PHYSICIAN'S OFFICE* E
I ask questions about things I don't understand	61.3%	60.3%	65.8%AB	64.7%B	67.8%AB
The invoice/bill I receive is easy to understand	70.6%CDE	70.8%	53.8%	56.0%	59.5%C
The people I interact with respect my privacy	64.5%B	57.0%	66.5%B	65.5B%	69.0%AB
The provider resolves any problems I express about my experience quickly	64.3%CDE	64.0%CDE	55.9%	44.4%	60.0%C
The invoice/bill I receive is consistent with my expectation	70.3%CDE	68.2%CDE	54.2%	55.0%	58.3%C
The provider explains things without making me feel rushed	61.6%	59.4%	61.8%	60.4%	66.6%ABCD
The people I interact with are knowledgeable	61.7%	60.4%	64.8%B	63.9%	67.4%AB
It's easy to resolve disputes I have about the value of the service I received	59.7%CDE	60.0%CDE	50.6%	50.9%	55.3%CD
The provider tries to make me feel satisfied with the service I received	66.3%CDE	64.4CD%	57.3%	56.3%	61.2%CD
I express dissatisfaction if I am unhappy with the service I received	61.2%CDE	58.6%C	54.3%	54.8%	56.8%
The check in process is easy	68.3%CD	65.7%CD	60.8%	60.6%	64.6%D
I know how much I have to pay for the service before I receive it	71.8%BCDE	64.8%CDE	52.3%	53.8%	56.7%C
The people I interact with make me feel welcome	69.3%CDE	67.4%CD	60.8%	60.0%	65.1%CD
The people I interact with are eager to serve me	64.8%CD	64.7%CD	59.3%	59.3%	63.9%CD
THE PROVIDER APPRECIATES MY BUSINESS	66.8%CDE	65.5%CDE	52.3%	53.2%	57.7%CD
The arrival experience is welcoming	66.8%BCDE	62.8%CD	54.9%	55.1%	59.3%CD
The provider makes me feel good about myself	56.3%	53.2%	54.2%	54.8%	59.3%BCD
The arrival environment is welcoming	64.8%CDE	62.0%CDE	55.0%	53.4%	57.2%
I can make an appointment/get a reservation when I want one	64.6%BCDE	60.2%CD	53.2%	53.5%	58.8%CD
I tell friends and family about experiences with the providers I visit/use	58.8%CD	59.9%CDE	53.8%	52.1%	55.6%
The provider know my preferences	50.6%BCD	42.3%	44.4%	44.2%	54.1%BCD
The people I interact with address me by name	48.3%AB	38.3%	50.5%B	50.3%B	60.9%ABCD
The provider asks for feedback about my experience after I leave	52.5%BCD	45.5%	47.0%	45.7%	48.6%
I review comments I find on social media about providers I am planning to visit/use	46.4%BCDE	41.5%CD	37.2%	36.3%	39.7%
	n=1200	n=1200	n=1200	n=1200	n=1200

*% agree, top three box on 10-point scale.

Capital letter = Significantly different than the percentage listed under the identified column at the 95% confidence level.

Figure A1: Service Variables Common to Hospitality and Healthcare.

OVERALL SENTIMENT	STAYING IN HOTEL/MOTEL/RESORT*	DINING OUT FOR LUNCH/DINNER*	VISITING A HOSPITAL*	VISITING A WALK-IN CLINIC*	VISITING A PHYSICIAN'S OFFICE*
COLUMN REFERENCE FOR TEST OF STATISTICAL SIGNIFICANCE AT 95% CONFIDENCE	A	B	C	D	E
I am generally satisfied with the overall experience I have with the providers I visit/use	69.4%CDE	67.1%CD	62.00%	58.30%	64.3%D
I am loyal to the providers I value/use	62.0%CD	61.1%CD	54.50%	51.80%	63.0%CD
I am generally satisfied with the service from the providers I visit/use	65.9%CD	64.3%CD	58.00%	55.90%	62.9%CD
I share my opinions about the providers I visit/use on social media	37.9%CD	37.7%CD	33.30%	33.30%	35.20%
I don't return to a provider from whom I received unsatisfactory service	68.9%CDE	67.7%CDE	57.80%	61.40%	62.1%C
	n=1200	n=1200	n=1200	n=1200	n=1200

% agree, top three box on 10-point scale.
Capital letter = Significantly different than the percentage listed under the identified column at the 95% confidence level.

Figure A2: Sentiment ratings of service quality.

RATER for Roger's Colonoscopy

Reliability

The following tactics may be used to remind the patient of the provider's reliability:

- On the answering machine, give the date of the received call, and roughly the time and date when the patient should expect a call back.

- Do not put the patient on hold listening to a looped message about "how valuable our patients are." Rather, offer the patient the opportunity to receive a call back without losing his/her place in line.

- Have most/all patient information completed by the patient prior to his/her arrival so at check-in the patient only needs to verify this information – not provide it once again.

Assurance

The following tactics maybe used to offer assurance to the patient.

- Have a list of patients, their arrival times, and photos available for the receptionist so when a patient checks in, the receptionist can welcome him/her by name, thank him/her for coming, and let him/her know they anticipated their arrival.

- Remind the patient of the doctor's/clinic's expertise in performing the procedure.
- Introduce the patient to all members of the team who will be involved with the procedure (either live or through a handout upon arrival).

Tangible

The following tactics/cues may be used by providers to make the service more tangible.

- Provide comfort blankets for the patient while he/she is awaiting the procedure.
- Introduce many of the servicescape elements discussed in Chapter 4 such as the use of relaxing colors, soft lighting, comfortable furniture, ambient music, aromatics, etc.
- Provide a clean, safe area for patient to put his/her clothes while having the procedure.

Empathy

The following tactics may be used to show empathy to the patient.

- Have the doctor and all other attending staff "see the person, within the patient" (i.e., talk to the patient as a person, acknowledge his/her fears, speak to him/her in layman's terms, etc.).
- Use a discrete method to alert patients seated in the common waiting room that the clinical team is ready to serve them (i.e., do not "shout" their name for all other patients to hear).

Responsiveness

The following tactics may be used to demonstrate responsiveness the patient.

- Have the doctor brief the caregiver on the preliminary results of the procedure immediately after its conclusion and express this in easily understood layman's terms.

- Provide the patient with a calendar of available dates/times to schedule the procedure so he/she may choose when it would be most convenient to schedule it, not be told when they need to come in.

- Answer all the patient's questions in layman's terms, not clinical terms.

- If procedure is scheduled to take place at a certain time, make sure the procedure occurs at that time, or keep the patient posted on the expected length of the delay prior to its commencement.

APPENDIX C

Customer Satisfaction Index Example

A N EXAMPLE OF HOW THE Customer Satisfaction Index (CSI) is calculated and used in practice by hospitality service providers is illustrated in the figures and table below.

	IMPORTANCE	BRAND A PERFORMANCE RATING	BRAND A IMPORTANCE x PERFORMANCE	BRAND B PERFORMANCE RATING	BRAND B IMPORTANCE x PERFORMANCE
	A	B	C	D	E
Feature	Scale: 1-10	Scale: 1-10	A*B	Scale: 1-10	A*D
It is a place friends like to go	7.3	7.6	55.48	6.4	46.72
Atmosphere is very pleasant	8.8	7.7	67.76	7.6	66.88
One place seems to have better odds	7.4	6.8	50.32	6.0	44.40
Slot machines filled in a timely manner	7.5	6.8	51	6.8	51.00
Type of promotions offered	7.4	7.7	56.98	6.8	50.32
Sum	38.4 (X 10 scale points = 384)		281.54		259.32
CSI Score			73.3 ((281.54/384) * 100)		67.5 ((259.32/384) * 100)

Figure B1: Index of competitive strength calculation.

The competitive advantages and disadvantages, which are shown in the matrix of competitive advantages, can be condensed into one single index: the index of competitive strength. All relative performances of the product on the individual factors are weighted with their importance and summed up.

Sum up the importance ratings for all features and multiply by the number of scale points – scale used was 1 to 10. (The numbers are in column A.)

For each attribute, multiply Average Importance x Average Performance. (Column C represents Importance x Performance for Brand A; Column E represents Importance x Performance for Brand B.)

Sum up all numbers in Column C and Column E.

Calculate the CSI as the total in Column C divided by the total in Column A (multiply by 100 to move decimal.) Repeat steps for competitors.

The table on the following page (Figure B2) illustrates CSI calculations for a hypothetical set of hotels in a major tourist destination.

The next figure illustrates how CSI scores may be plotted against the average rate of each hotel and reveals how one hotel is priced vis-à-vis the others and how the corresponding CSI scores compare:

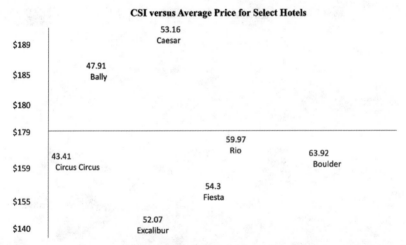

The calculated index for each property is shown on the X axis and the average price is shown on the Y axis. This allows one to gain an understanding of how one property is priced vis-à-vis other properties relative to their CSI score. For example, Boulder has a CSI of 63.92 – the best of all properties. Yet, it is priced below the average. Given the price of Caesar and Bally with lower CSI scores, Boulder could probably raise its prices.

Figure B3: CSI average rate plot.

	FEEL SAFE THERE	FRIENDLY STAFF	PLACE MY FRIENDS LIKE TO GO	ALWAYS HAVE GOOD ENTERTAINMENT	DRINK ORDERS TAKEN IN TIMELY MANNER	CASHIER LINES ARE SHORT	RESTAURANTS OFFER GREAT VALUE	CAN GET CHANGE QUICKLY	SLOT MACHINES FILLED IN TIMELY MANNER	LIKE THE PROMOTION OFFERED	YOU GET FREE THINGS	OVERALL AVERAGE	RATE	CSI
IMPORTANCE	8.20	8.20	6.27	4.80	6.12	6.37	7.49	6.33	5.67	4.80	6.15	6.40		
RIO	7.26	6.60	6.49	6.47	5.93	5.91	5.70	5.54	5.35	4.96	5.93		$179.00	60.0
BALLY'S	6.55	5.28	3.96	4.59	5.11	5.05	4.05	4.70	4.60	3.75	4.20	4.71	$185.00	47.9
BOULDER	7.40	6.88	6.40	5.74	6.50	5.90	6.54	6.11	5.89	6.16	6.32		$160.00	63.9
CAESAR'S	7.19	5.85	6.15	5.81	5.37	5.43	4.32	4.82	5.07	3.62	5.24		$189.00	53.2
CIRCUS CIRCUS	4.70	4.60	4.07	4.24	4.59	4.63	4.55	4.15	4.21	3.80	4.30		$159.00	43.4
EXCALIBUR	6.61	5.64	5.01	4.89	5.03	5.42	5.01	5.19	5.04	4.06	5.12		$140.00	52.1
FIESTA	6.19	6.00	4.75	4.64	5.48	5.4	5.61	5.60	5.34	4.66	5.25	5.36	$155.00	54.3

	Rate	CSi
Rio	$179.00	59.97
Bally	$185.00	47.81
Boulder	$160.00	63.92
Caesar	$189.00	53.16
Circus Circus	$159.00	43.41
Excalibur	$140.00	52.07
Fiesta	$155.00	54.3

Respondents rated the relative importance of each attribute when selecting a casino hotel on a 10-point scale (1 = "not at all important" to 10 = "very important").
For example, the attribute "cashier lines are short" received an average importance rating of 6.37. Respondents then rated the extent to which the attributes
described each hotel on a 10-point scale (1 = "does not describe the hotel at all" to 10 = "describes the hotel perfectly").

Figure B2: CSI calculation example.

.